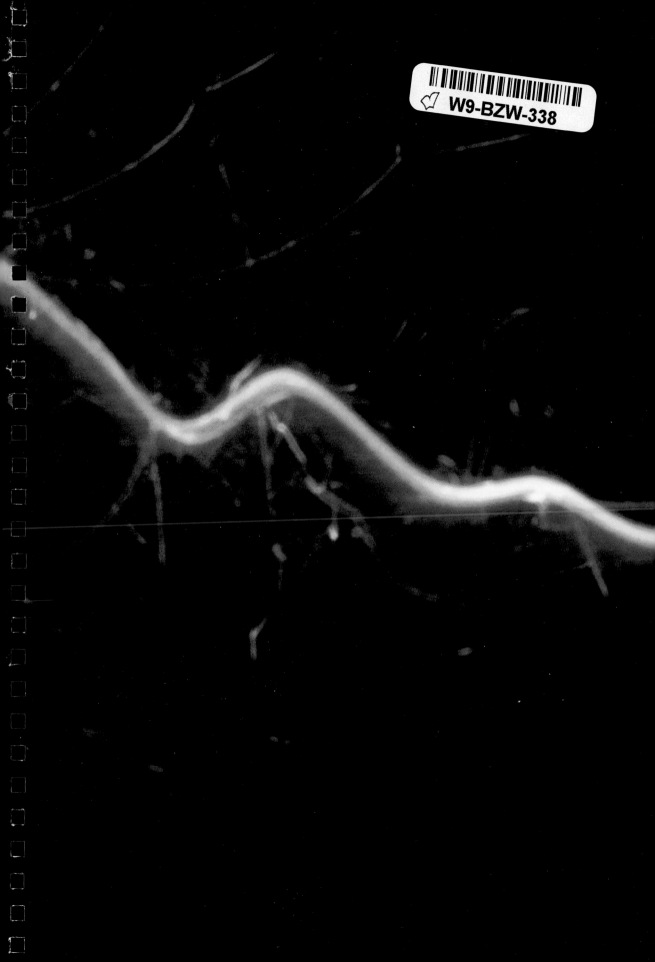

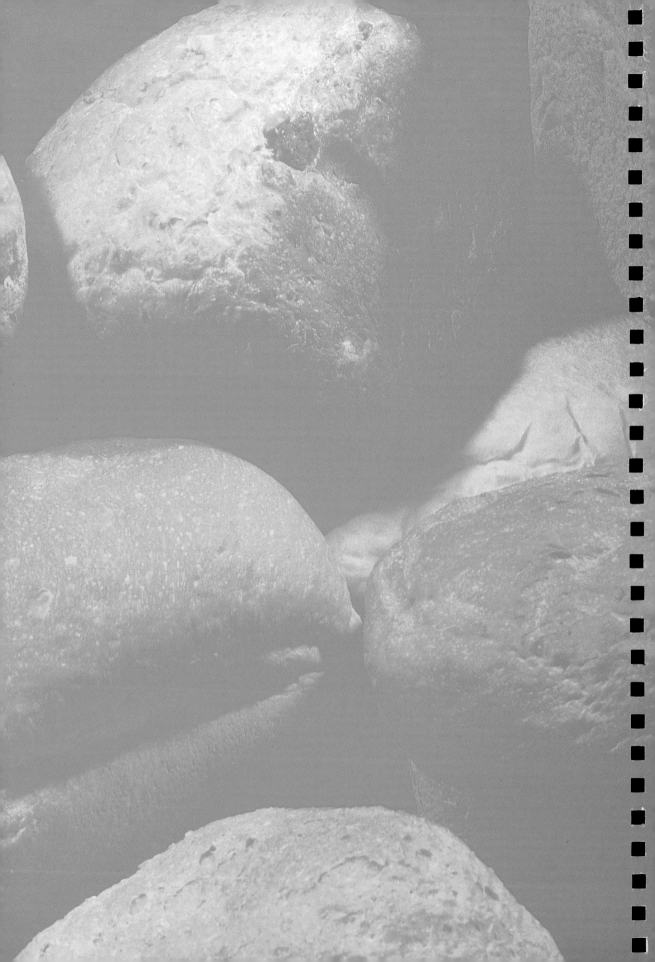

BREAD®

electric

Innovative Cooking Enterprises

I.C.E., Inc. Anchorage, Alaska

Developed by:
INNOVATIVE COOKING ENTERPRISES * I.C.E., INC.

Cover, Book Design & Photography by:
ART & INTERNATIONAL PRODUCTIONS
SASHA SAGAN & JIM TILLY

Written by:
SUZAN NIGHTINGALE

Published by: Innovative Cooking Enterprises * I.C.E., Inc.
P. O. Box 240888
Anchorage, Alaska 99524-0888

SAN 297-441X

First Printing,   August, 1991, Second Printing, November, 1991;
Revised, June 1992, Fourth Printing, December 1992;
Revised, June 1993; Sixth Printing, September 1994,
Seventh Printing, December 1994; Eighth Printing,
January, 1995; Ninth Printing, November, 1996.
Second Edition, Tenth Printing, September, 1997

Printed in China

Library of Congress Catalog Card Number: 91-72650

ISBN 0-9629831-7-7

Table of Contents

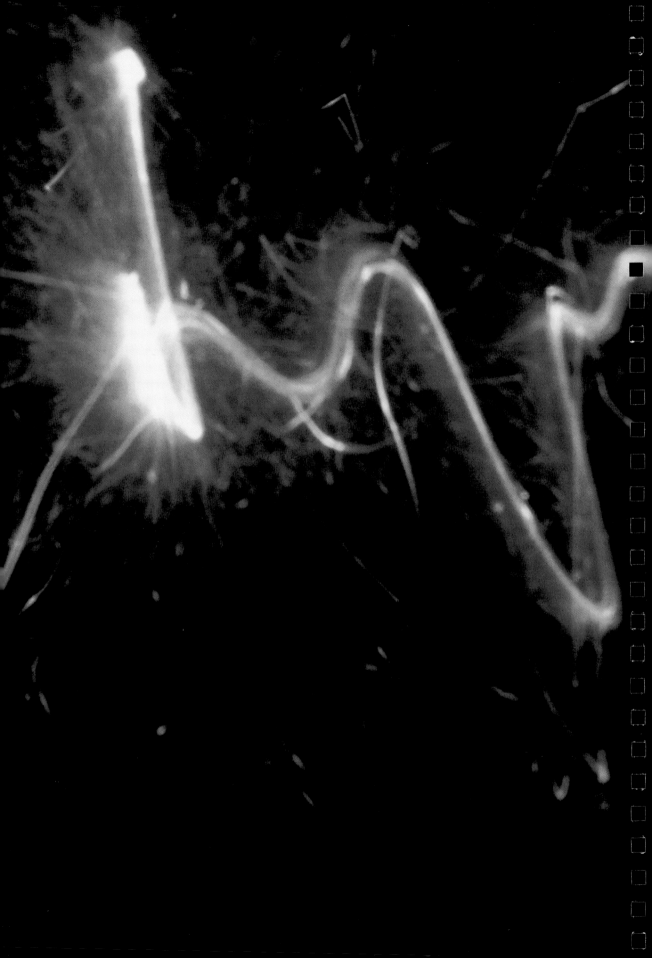

ELECTRIC BREAD, YOUR MACHINE & INGREDIENTS

Welcome to *Electric Bread* - recipes for people with more taste than time. We've baked over 25,000 loaves to ensure our recipes work in every bread machine, and made some important discoveries along the way. Come into our kitchen... and we'll tell you what we've learned.

Every chef has a secret ingredient, and we'll tell you ours — our test kitchen. With more than 200 bread machines humming around the clock, ours is the only kitchen working directly with every machine manufacturer and major flour and yeast producer. Our on-going research ensures that **ELECTRIC BREAD** keeps abreast of the latest developments in technology and ingredients.

Our test kitchen began with bread machine owners like you. All of us had favorite recipes, but none worked in every machine.

The secret of our success - the Test Kitchen working with new bread machines, flour and yeast to ensure our information is up to date.

After searching in vain for a source of "universal" recipes, we decided to create a company, start a test kitchen, and publish our own recipe book.

Maybe it was the long Alaskan winter. Or maybe it was our conviction that it *was possible* to develop recipes to work well in all machines.

Our goal then was the same as now: every recipe had to produce *quality bread* in every model on the market. No doorstops, no fluffy exploding loaves, no toasted cardboard — quality bread every time.

And in spite of the dramatic changes in technology, flours and yeast, we've done it again and again. Over 25,000 loaves later, our company continues to test our recipes and provide personalized recipe support toll free at **1-800-541-2733**.

So start baking. You will find our recipes are so easy, so flavorful and so much fun, they beg you to come out and play. Enjoy!

OUR RECIPES HAVE BEEN TESTED IN THESE MACHINES:

American Harvest • Aroma • Betty Crocker • Black & Decker • Breadman • Chefmate
Charlescraft • Circulair • Citizen • Dak • Franklin • Goldstar • Hitachi • Kenmore
Mister Loaf • MK Sieko • Mr Coffee • National • Oster
Panasonic • Pillsbury • Proctor-Silex • Red Star • Regal
Salton-Maxim • Sanyo • Sunbeam • Toastmaster • Welbilt
West Bend • Williams-Sonoma • Zojirushi & others...

TIPS FOR SUCCESS

Each recipe contains specific hints. These tips apply to every machine and recipe.

MEASURING

Bread machines don't ask much of the home baker, but they do require one thing: precision. Careful measurements can make the difference between a luscious loaf and a disappointing dud. For dry ingredients scoop into a regulation measuring cup and tap once lightly to settle contents. Make certain the top is level – a heaping cup can be a cup-and-a-half if you're not careful. Key ingredients - like yeast, salt and sugar - use small exact quantities. Tableware doesn't cut it when accuracy counts. So use standard measuring spoons with ingredients leveled off. Use clear measuring cups for liquids. Set the cup on a counter and check at eye level to make sure you're on the mark. When using an egg in our recipes, break the egg into the measuring cup and then fill with water to the recipe's combined egg and water measurement.

RECIPE SIZE

Each *Electric Bread* Gourmet Bread recipe gives the ingredients for a Regular, a Large, and an Extra Large loaf. Which recipe you use depends on your machine. The capacity of a bread machine refers to its pan size. With a liquid measuring cup, determine how many cups of water your machine's pan holds when filled to the rim. Then use the tested recipe size shown below for your pan capacity.

Pan Capacity	Recipe Size
Less than 12 cups	Regular
12 to 16 cups	Large
More than 16 cups	Extra Large

Our Specialty Doughs provide two recipe sizes ...A and B...to allow you to match the bread quantity to your serving needs. Size A is for machines with less than 12 cups of pan capacity. In larger capacity machines, you may prepare either size A or B.

WATER TEMPERATURE

Use tepid water in your machine. Cold water won't activate the yeast, hot water will speed it too much, and very hot water will kill it.

A Good Start

Load ingredients in the order suggested in your owner's manual. For consistency's sake, all of our recipes list the liquids first and yeast last. Because moisture activates the yeast, you don't want your yeast contacting the liquid ahead of time – especially on a delay bake. Load dried fruits, vegetables and spices away from liquid ingredients so

they don't soak up the water and sabotage the liquid/flour ratio. During the first knead "lift the hood" and make sure all the ingredients were pulled into the dough ball by the kneading blade. This is also a good time to check the dough. Unless otherwise stated, the dough ball should be round, smooth-textured, soft and tacky to the touch.

Extra Knead

For those machines without a French, whole wheat, or whole grain cycle, we developed the "extra knead" technique to give bread structure. Simply start your machine and let it go through the first knead, then stop and restart it from the beginning again. For even lighter results using heavier flours, allow the dough to rise before restarting your machine.

Spoilage

Store yeast in a cool, dry, airtight container. Each yeast has its own shelf life, but once opened, all yeast should be stored in the refrigerator. Never use perishable ingredients – milk, yogurt, meat, cheese, eggs – in a delay bake cycle. Left unrefrigerated, these ingredients can spoil before the baking process even starts.

Fruit

Always drain canned fruits well to keep an accurate liquid/flour ratio. When using dried fruit, remember that older fruit has a more concentrated sugar content; too much may overactivate the yeast. Beware of fruit (such as apricots) treated with sulfur dioxide; this preservative can kill the yeast.

Machine Cycles

Cycle lengths and names vary significantly between machines. *Electric Bread* recipes were formulated to work on the cycles common to all machines, using the cycle names recommended by the Bread Machine Industry Association. Cycles listed under Success Hints mean that particular recipe worked in all machines using those cycles. Try the cycles we suggest first, then experiment with other cycles on your machine.

LOAF SIZE AND TEXTURE

One of the most frequent comments we receive on our customer service line is: "My bread didn't turn out right." Many have wrestled with disappointment over a loaf's appearance only to find out later that it wasn't a failure at all, and their loaf was supposed to be that way.

Different kinds of bread have different textures and heights because they are made of different ingredients. Our Pumpernickel recipe, for example, produces a shorter, denser loaf than Saffron. As a general rule, whole wheat flours produce a denser loaf than lighter flours. Some people like a chewier texture for sandwiches, others want their sandwich breads light and fluffy.

Comparative Loaf Size
Saffron (left) and Pumpernickel

Because different people like different bread, the guide on the following page indicates the relative size and texture of our *Electric Bread* recipes. Each recipe has a relative rating between 1 and 5. Pumpernickel (with a rating of 1) is a smaller, compact loaf with a denser texture. Saffron (with a rating of 5) is a large, light, airy loaf with a delicate texture.

As you can see, *Electric Bread* brings you a wide variety to choose from. Use the Loaf Size and Texture Guide on the next page to evaluate your loaf results or to select recipes with the texture you prefer.

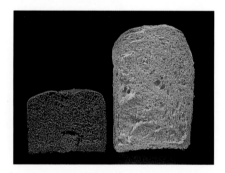

Comparative Loaf Texture
Pumpernickel (left) and Saffron

NUTRITIONAL INFORMATION

For the nutrition conscious baker, each recipe provides per serving calories, cholesterol and sodium content and the percentage of protein, carbohydrates and fat. *Electric Bread* nutritional information is based on 12 servings for a Gourmet Bread Large recipe and a two ounce serving of the Specialty Dough Size A recipe.

LOAF SIZE & TEXTURE GUIDE

Bread Recipe & Page Number	1	2	3	4	5
Almond Poppy, 52				■	
Apple Oat, 42			■		
Apricot, 86			■		
Baked Potato, 76		■			
Banana Granola, 118	■				
Bits o' Bacon, 72				■	
Bleu Cheese & Port, 114				■	
Cajun Spice, 50				■	
Carrot, 68				■	
Certainly Citrus, 46					■
Challah, 82					■
Cherry Yogurt, 24					■
Chocolate Cherry, 104		■			
Cinco de Mayo, 22					■
Classic White, 26					■
Cottage Dill, 48				■	
100% Crunch, 78	■				
Easy French, 62					■
Fall Harvest, 106				■	
Garden Herb, 80				■	
Garlic, 56				■	
Greek Isle, 110					■
Health Grain, 20		■			
Honey Mustard, 40				■	
Honey Wheat, 54				■	
Italian Wheat, 70					■

Bread Recipe & Page Number	1	2	3	4	5
Kulich, 36				■	
Light Rye, 64				■	
Luscious Luau, 94					■
Maraschino Pecan, 60					■
Mocha Java, 84				■	
Multi-Grain & More, 38					■
Nutty Coconut, 100					■
Onion, 90					■
Outrageously Oatmeal, 102				■	
Peaches & Cream, 98					■
Peanut Butter, 44		■			
Pizza Pleasure, 96					■
Pumpernickel, 88		■			
Raisin Bread, 28	■				
Rum Raisin, 92				■	
Saffron, 58					■
Saucy Apple, 74				■	
Sourdough White, 116	■				
Sun Nut, 112				■	
Swedish Limpa, 32				■	
Sweet Coconut Curry, 66				■	
Tabouli, 108				■	
Tangy Cranberry, 120		■			
Tropical Medley, 34		■			
100% Whole Wheat, 30				■	

This chart gives a relative rating, ranging from 1 to 5, for each *Electric Bread* recipe. The number 1 indicates the densest loaves and 5 the lightest.

Our executive chef likes to say that cooking is an art but baking is a science. He doesn't mean you have to be Einstein to bake bread, just that basic chemistry is what turns flour and yeast into bread.

The ingredients work off one another in a precise way, and slight mismeasurements - or inappropriate ingredients - can throw off that critical balance.

Flour, for instance, isn't just "flour" anymore. Different flours are made from particular wheats for distinct uses, and they produce dramatically different results in home bakeries. Pastry, cake and many all-purpose flours don't work with yeast the way bread flour does.

Good bread flours include hard wheats that have the high protein/high gluten content needed to give bread good structure. Take the time to cruise the flour aisles in your markets, read some labels, and note the products that specify they are formulated especially for bread.

One of the great things about home bakeries is that you don't need a Ph.D. in Yeast to make quality bread. The machines conquer the mystique of yeast with the push of a button. Still, a short explanation will help take the mystery out of what's going on behind that closed lid or door.

Yeast is a living organism. Mixed with water and sugar, the yeast wakes up during the kneading process and gives off carbon dioxide bubbles, filling your bread with tiny holes that make it rise. (That's why a high protein, high gluten flour is important; the gluten is what works with the gas to achieve the right structure.)

Most recipes contain sugar in some form - not for sweetness but to jump-start the yeast and to promote browning. Salt, on the other hand, inhibits the yeast, but is needed for flavor - a balance to keep in mind as you experiment with sugary fruits or salty meats in your bread machine.

Because bread is the result of this chemical reaction, *precise measurements are vital.* Grandma may have been able to eyeball her flour, but bread machines are designed for consistently measured ingredients.

In the following pages, we talk about some of the ingredients we used in our test kitchen. But remember, geographic regions often have different brands and sometimes their own regional mills. It's worth the investment for you to buy several types and experiment with your own machine, comparing loaf height, texture and taste from the same basic recipe. If you bake several loaves back-to-back, you'll spot the differences.

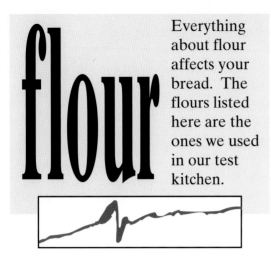

flour

Everything about flour affects your bread. The flours listed here are the ones we used in our test kitchen.

BAKERS & CHEF - For bakers looking for bread flour in larger quantities, Bakers & Chef offers its enriched bleached bread flour in 25lb. bags. Made from a blend of hard spring and winter wheat, Bakers & Chefs can be found at Sam's warehouse clubs.

GOLD MEDAL - General Mills provides a variety of flour products from hard and soft wheats. Widely available, Gold Medal's Better for Bread Flour is blended from a selection of high protein flours. The new wheat blend, used in place of regular bread flour, gives a light wheat taste to favorite recipes. These finely milled flours produced a soft, airy bread with a crisp, flaky crust.

ROGERS - These blended Canadian bread flours are milled using only hard red spring wheat. Rogers consistently produced flavorful loaves with excellent crust and texture.

ROBIN HOOD -These new bread flours were shipped to us from Canada where they are available nationwide. Milled from unique blends of Canadian hard wheats, Robin Hood produced pleasant, even textured loaves with subtle flavor.

PILLSBURY - Available nationwide, Pillsbury is known for the consistent quality of its baking products. Pillsbury's BEST Bread Flour is a finely milled flour that produces a light, fluffy loaf with a slight sweetness in taste. The Whole Wheat flour also produced consistent flavorful loaves.

ARROWHEAD MILLS - Located on the high plains of the Texas Panhandle, Arrowhead Mills makes its all-natural flour from hard red winter wheat grown without insecticides or herbicides. Unbleached, this consistent performer baked a sturdy, flavorful loaf with a soft golden glow. Arrowhead Mills products are distributed nationwide.

The test kitchen also baked our recipes with a variety of other flours, including those manufactured by Five Roses of Canada, ConAgra, Dakota Mills, King Arthur, Hodgson Mills and Stone-Buhr.

yeast

The rise and fall of great bread can be traced to the right yeast with the right flour.

If flour is the foundation of your bread, yeast is the primary building block. We used powdered yeasts - both the fast rise and the active dry - for their convenience and efficiency. Some yeasts enhance the flavor of your flour, while others impart a distinctive flavor of their own. And some yeasts work better with certain kinds of flours than others in bread machines. If you're using a heavier flour, and you want a lighter bread, try increasing the yeast by 1/8 teaspoon at a time.

RED STAR - RED STAR Yeast & Products, a Division of Universal Foods Corporation, manufactures Active Dry, QUICK•RISE and bread machine yeasts. Available in convenient packages and vacuum-packed jars, we liked using RED STAR yeasts with light, finer milled flours.

FLEISCHMANN'S - Widely available, Fleischmann's is known throughout the world of baking. The Active Dry yeast varieties consistently produced a sturdy texture with uniform shape and air pocket distribution. We liked the Bread Machine yeast best in the more complex breads with multiple ingredients and flavors.

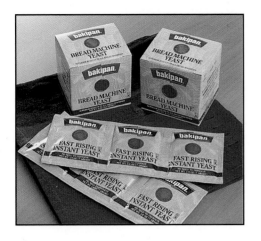

BAKIPAN - This fast-rising yeast is available in Canada, and in select grocery stores in the U.S. In our test loaves, it produced a uniform, springy texture. With no distracting yeast taste, Bakipan enhanced the natural flavor of the flour itself. Bakipan can also be ordered by mail at (800) 665-0991.

SAF - Made in France, this fast rise yeast has long been a favorite of professional bakers. Its strength and forgiving nature make it ideal for home bakers, too. An instant favorite of our test kitchen staff, SAF is available in select grocery and gourmet specialty stores or by calling SAF at (800) 411-5149.

spices
Freshness and quality are key to premium flavor.

SPICE ISLAND - Established in 1941, this is the only national brand of gourmet spices that grows herbs on its own farms in California in addition to importing select spices from around the world. Offering a high quality and complete gourmet seasoning assortment, Spice Island is conveniently available at most grocery stores.

We also tested with other spices and ingredients, including Morton & Bassett salt-free spices and Chef Paul Prudhomme's Magic Seasoning Blends' Seafood Magic, the flavorful fire in our Cajun Bread.

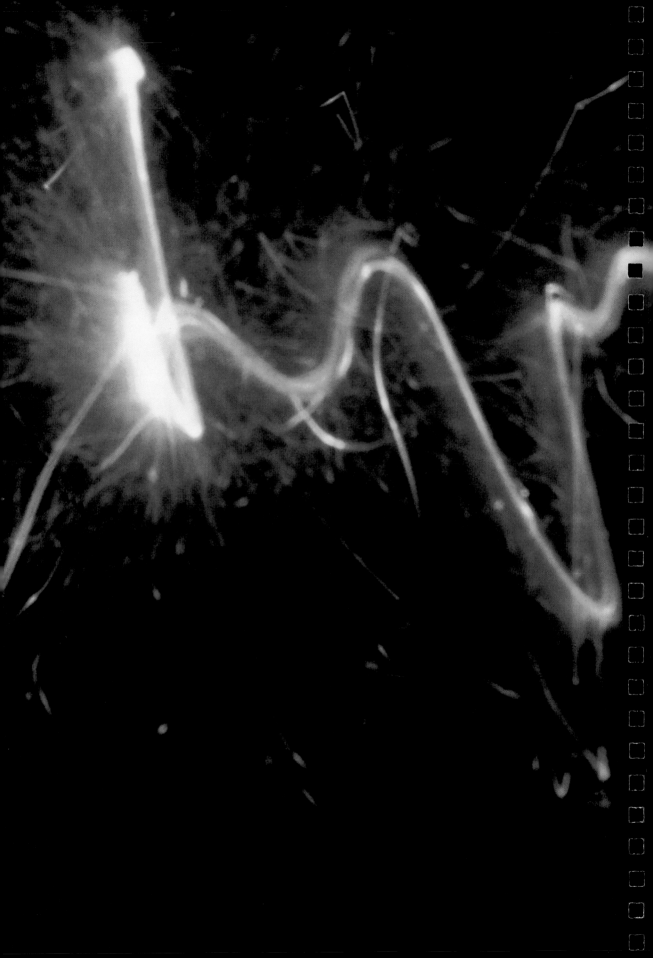

GOURMET BREADS

One does not live by bread alone - but you might try it with our 51 gourmet recipes. From the heartiest Health Grain to the lightest Luscious Luau, you'll find a loaf for every occasion. And best of all, they're yours with the push of a button!

Health Grain

Calories 211
Cholesterol 0 mg.
Sodium 277 mg.
Protein 13 %
Carbohydrates 65 %
Fat 26 %

Nutritional information per serving

Who said good health can't taste good? This bread has everything, including flavor. Moist with a light crunch, our Health Grain is chock full of good things. But you don't have to tell the finicky eaters about the bran or the wheat germ. Serve this with a fresh fruit plate, and let them think it's all about taste.

Success Hints

- For a change of pace, replace sunflower seeds with pumpkin seeds.

- This recipe can be used with the white, rapid, or delay bake cycles.

REGULAR	LARGE	EXTRA LARGE
Water		
3/4 cup	1 1/4 cups	1 1/2 cups
Carrots *freshly grated or chopped*		
1/4 cup	1/2 cups	1/2 cup
Honey		
2 tsp.	1 Tbsp.	1 1/2 Tbsp.
Olive Oil		
1 Tbsp.	2 Tbsp.	2 Tbsp.
White Bread Flour		
1 1/2 cups	2 cups	3 cups
Whole Wheat Flour		
1/4 cup	3/4 cup	1/2 cup
Dry Milk		
2 tsp.	1 Tbsp.	1 Tbsp.
Salt		
1 tsp.	1 1/2 tsp.	2 tsp.
Bran Flakes		
1/4 cup	1/2 cup	1/2 cup
Wheat Germ		
1 Tbsp.	2 Tbsp.	2 Tbsp.
Raisins		
1/4 cup	1/2 cup	1/2 cup
Sunflower Seeds		
1/4 cup	1/2 cup	1/2 cup
Yeast *fast rise*		
1 tsp.	2 tsp.	2 tsp.
- or -		
Yeast *active dry*		
2 tsp.	2 tsp.	2 tsp.

Cinco de Mayo

Calories 180
Cholesterol 0 mg.
Sodium 297 mg.

Protein 11 %
Carbohydrates 78 %
Fat 10 %

Nutritional information per serving

Our Cinco de Mayo bread was inspired by Mexico's May 5th national holiday, but don't wait until then to try it! The jalapeño pepper and cilantro create a fiesta of flavor that's perfect for brisk fall weekends and cold winter nights. Served with chili, this lightly textured loaf will convince you never to go back to plain corn bread again. *Buen Apetito!*

Success Hints

- If you want a little more zip, increase jalapeño peppers to taste.

- Drain canned chilies, corn and jalapeño peppers well. Be careful! Jalapeño and chili juice can sting. Be sure to wash your hands after preparation.

- This bread is a great party bread because of its unexpected texture and flavor.

- This recipe can be used with the white and rapid bake cycles.

REGULAR	LARGE	EXTRA LARGE
Water		
2/3 cup	1 cup	1 1/3 cups
Olive Oil		
2 tsp.	1 Tbsp.	4 tsp.
Whole Kernel Corn		
1/3 cup	1/2 cup	2/3 cup
Green Chilies canned/diced		
2 Tbsp.	1/4 cup	1/4 cup
Jalapeño Peppers canned/diced		
1 tsp.	1/2 Tbsp.	2 tsp.
Lemon Juice		
1/4 tsp.	1/4 tsp.	1/4 tsp.
White Bread Flour		
2 cups	3 cups	4 cups
Sugar		
1 Tbsp.	1 1/2 Tbsp.	2 Tbsp.
Salt		
1 tsp.	1 1/2 tsp.	2 tsp.
Corn Meal		
1/2 cup	3/4 cup	1 cup
Cumin		
1 tsp.	2 tsp.	2 tsp.
Yeast fast rise		
1 1/2 tsp.	1 1/2 tsp.	1 1/2 tsp.
- or - **Yeast** active dry		
2 tsp.	2 tsp.	2 tsp.

Cherry Yogurt

Calories 169   Protein 12 %
Cholesterol 0 mg.   Carbohydrates 83 %
Sodium 232 mg.   Fat 4 %

Nutritional information per serving

This sweet bread, featuring choice dried Bing cherries, is surprisingly versatile. You can use it in lieu of raisin bread for French toast, or serve it warm with cream cheese and honey for a dessert bread. The applesauce and yogurt contribute a refreshing moistness to this light loaf.

REGULAR	LARGE	EXTRA LARGE
Water		
1/2 cup	3/4 cup	1 cup
Cherry Yogurt		
low fat		
1/3 cup	1/2 cup	3/4 cup
Applesauce		
unsweetened		
2 Tbsp.	1/4 cup	1/4 cup
White Bread Flour		
2 cups	3 cups	4 cups
Brown Sugar		
1 Tbsp.	1 1/2 Tbsp.	2 Tbsp.
Salt		
3/4 tsp.	1 1/4 tsp.	1 1/2 tsp.
Cherries		
dried		
1/2 cup	3/4 cup	1 cup
Yeast		
fast rise		
1 tsp.	1 1/2 tsp.	2 tsp.
- or -		
Yeast		
active dry		
2 tsp.	2 1/2 tsp.	3 tsp.

Success Hints

- We used Chukar brand cherries, available in our accessories section and gourmet food stores.

- Use low fat fruited yogurt.

- Add the dried cherries whole.

- This recipe can be used with the white or rapid bake cycles.

24

Classic White

Calories 157
Cholesterol 6 mg.
Sodium 297 mg.

Protein 13 %
Carbohydrates 71 %
Fat 15 %

Nutritional information per serving

	REGULAR	LARGE	EXTRA LARGE
Water	3/4 cup	1 cup	1 1/4 cups
Butter	1 Tbsp.	2 Tbsp.	2 Tbsp.
White Bread Flour	2 cups	3 cups	4 cups
Dry Milk	1 Tbsp.	1 1/2 Tbsp.	2 Tbsp.
Sugar	1 1/2 Tbsp.	2 Tbsp.	3 Tbsp.
Salt	1 tsp.	1 1/2 tsp.	2 tsp.
Yeast *fast rise*	1 tsp.	1 3/4 tsp.	1 3/4 tsp.
- or - **Yeast** *active dry*	1 1/2 tsp.	2 tsp.	2 tsp.

This is a classic - plain white bread, but a world away from store bought. This loaf's light bodied texture makes it the standard for sandwich breads or the perfect accompaniment for meals. Bake it while you're still deciding what's for dinner; like most classics, its versatility lies in its simplicity.

Success Hints

■ Classic White makes great low fat croutons. Lightly butter bread slices, cube, and bake at 350° until crisp.

■ Classic White is the perfect bread for sampling the savory and sweet spreads on pages 142 - 143.

■ This recipe can be made with the white, rapid, or delay bake cycles.

Raisin Bread

Calories 194   Protein 12 %
Cholesterol 6 mg.   Carbohydrates 78 %
Sodium 300 mg.   Fat 14 %

Nutritional information per serving

Raisin bread is one of life's simple pleasures - and just about everyone's all-time favorite breakfast bread. Our recipe blends the fruit right into the loaf unless you add the raisins in mid-cycle; it's your choice. Either way, this promises to be one of your best breads for French toast.

Success Hints

□ For whole raisins in the bread, add fruit at the beep on the fruit and nut cycle or after the first knead.

□ If using the rapid bake cycle, add raisins with other ingredients.

□ For a real taste delight, try with our Honey Butter spread - page 143.

□ This recipe can be made with the white, rapid, or delay bake cycles.

	REGULAR	LARGE	EXTRA LARGE
Water	3/4 cup	1 cup	1 1/3 cups
Butter	1 Tbsp.	2 Tbsp.	2 Tbsp.
White Bread Flour	2 cups	3 cups	4 cups
Dry Milk	1 Tbsp.	2 Tbsp.	2 Tbsp.
Sugar	1 Tbsp.	1 1/2 Tbsp.	2 Tbsp.
Salt	1 tsp.	1 1/2 tsp.	2 tsp.
Cinnamon	1/2 tsp.	1 tsp.	1 tsp.
Raisins	1/2 cup	1 cup	1 cup
Yeast *fast rise*	1 1/2 tsp.	2 tsp.	2 tsp.
- or -			
Yeast *active dry*	2 tsp.	3 tsp.	3 tsp.

100% Whole Wheat

Calories 164   Protein 17 %
Cholesterol 6 mg.   Carbohydrates 75 %
Sodium 300 mg.   Fat 16 %

Nutritional information per serving

REGULAR	LARGE	EXTRA LARGE
Water		
1 cup	1 1/4 cups	1 1/3 cups
Butter		
1 1/2 Tbsp.	2 Tbsp.	2 Tbsp.
Honey		
1 1/4 Tbsp.	2 Tbsp.	2 Tbsp.
Molasses		
2 tsp.	1 Tbsp.	2 Tbsp.
Whole Wheat Flour		
2 1/2 cups	3 1/2 cups	4 cups
Dry Milk		
1 1/4 Tbsp.	2 Tbsp.	2 Tbsp.
Salt		
1 tsp.	1 1/2 tsp.	2 tsp.
Gluten		
1 Tbsp.	1 1/2 Tbsp.	1 1/2 Tbsp.
Yeast *fast rise*		
1 1/2 tsp.	1 1/2 tsp.	1 1/2 tsp.
- or -		
Yeast *active dry*		
2 tsp.	2 1/2 tsp.	2 1/2 tsp.

The trick to making 100% whole wheat bread is extra kneading time, which gives the yeast and gluten time to create a lighter loaf. Many manufacturers produce home bakeries with a special whole wheat cycle; if your machine doesn't have one, our extra knead method described on page 9 works as an easy alternative.

Success Hints

- The gluten gives the whole wheat flour the structure necessary for a good loaf. If your market doesn't stock wheat gluten, try your local health food store.

- This recipe can be made with the whole wheat, white or the delay bake cycle.

Swedish Limpa

Calories 169   Protein 12 %
Cholesterol 6 mg.   Carbohydrates 73 %
Sodium 300 mg.   Fat 14 %

Nutritional information per serving

This rich but light rye is the corner-stone of a traditional Swedish break-fast. The anise and orange peel add just a kiss of flavor to complement the rye. Our Swedish friend, Carina Saunders, says to serve limpa with a slice of cheese, a soft-boiled egg in an egg cup, and a cup of strong black coffee. *Ja!*

Success Hints

- We produced our flat ale by opening a dark beer and stirring until the bubbles were dispersed. Scoop off residual foam before measuring ale.

- This recipe can be made with the white or rapid bake cycles.

REGULAR	LARGE	EXTRA LARGE
Water		
1/4 cup	1/2 cup	1/2 cup
Butter		
1 Tbsp.	2 Tbsp.	2 Tbsp.
Honey		
3/4 Tbsp.	1 Tbsp.	1 1/2 Tbsp.
Molasses		
3/4 Tbsp.	1 Tbsp.	1 1/2 Tbsp.
Flat Ale		
1/2 cup	3/4 cup	1 cup
White Bread Flour		
1 3/4 cups	2 1/2 cups	3 1/2 cups
Rye Flour		
1/4 cup	1/2 cup	1/2 cup
Dry Milk		
1 Tbsp.	2 Tbsp.	2 Tbsp.
Salt		
1 tsp.	1 1/2 tsp.	2 tsp.
Cardamon		
1/4 tsp.	1/2 tsp.	1/2 tsp.
Anise Seed		
1/4 tsp.	1/2 tsp.	1/2 tsp.
Orange Peel		
1 1/2 tsp.	1 Tbsp.	1 Tbsp.
Yeast *fast rise*		
1 tsp.	2 tsp.	2 tsp.
- or -		
Yeast *active dry*		
2 tsp.	3 tsp.	3 1/2 tsp.

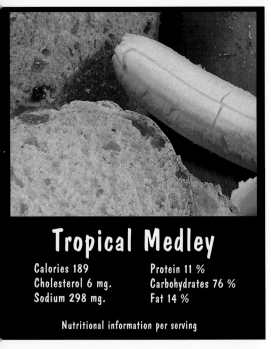

Tropical Medley

Calories 189
Cholesterol 6 mg.
Sodium 298 mg.

Protein 11 %
Carbohydrates 76 %
Fat 14 %

Nutritional information per serving

This is a light, colorful bread full of fruity surprises. Because of the variety in the dried fruit mix, each bite has a different flavor. Moms love this bread for its wholesomeness and kids love it for its natural sweetness.

Success Hints

- Apricots, coconut, golden raisins, papaya and pineapple make a good combination for the dried fruit mix.

- Several brands of pre-chopped and pre-packaged "Tropical Medley" mix are available – great for fast preparation.

- You don't need to use the fruit and nut cycle; simply add the dried fruit with your other ingredients.

- This recipe can be made with the white, rapid or delay bake cycles.

REGULAR	LARGE	EXTRA LARGE
Water		
3/4 cup	1 1/8 cups	1 1/2 cups
Butter		
1 Tbsp.	2 Tbsp.	3 Tbsp.
White Bread Flour		
2 cups	3 cups	4 cups
Dry Milk		
1 Tbsp.	2 Tbsp.	3 Tbsp.
Sugar		
1 1/2 tsp.	2 tsp.	1 Tbsp.
Salt		
1 tsp.	1 1/2 tsp.	2 tsp.
Dried Fruit Mix *chopped*		
1/2 cup	1 cup	1 1/2 cups
Yeast *fast rise*		
1 tsp.	1 1/2 tsp.	2 tsp.
- or -		
Yeast *active dry*		
2 tsp.	2 tsp.	3 tsp.

Kulich

Calories 203
Cholesterol 18 mg.
Sodium 292 mg.

Protein 12 %
Carbohydrates 76 %
Fat 12 %

Nutritional information per serving

Sasha, our photographer, says that in Russia, this traditional Easter bread is baked in small loaves and given for good luck to friends who come to visit. Your visitors will think they're lucky, too, if you serve this festive loaf. Topped with the traditional sweet Paskha, it's one of our brunch favorites *any* day of the year.

Success Hints

- Break egg into liquid measuring cup, then fill with water to the combined egg and water measurement.

- For a glazed finish, brush bread while still hot with a mixture of 1 Tbsp. each of honey, lemon juice and triple sec.

- We used a combination of mixed dried cherries, apples, apricots and prunes.

- This recipe can be baked using the white or rapid bake cycles.

REGULAR	LARGE	EXTRA LARGE
1 Egg plus Water to equal		
5/8 cup	3/4 cup	1 cup
Milk		
2 Tbsp.	1/4 cup	1/4 cup
Honey		
2 Tbsp.	2 Tbsp.	3 Tbsp.
Vanilla Extract		
3/4 tsp.	1 tsp.	1 tsp.
White Bread Flour		
2 cups	3 cups	3 3/4 cups
Salt		
1 tsp.	1 1/2 tsp.	1 1/2 tsp.
Raisins		
2 Tbsp.	1/4 cup	1/4 cup
Mixed Dried Fruit		
1/4 cup	1/2 cup	1/2 cup
Lemon Peel *dried*		
1/4 tsp.	1/2 tsp.	1/2 tsp.
Toasted Almonds		
2 Tbsp.	1/4 cup	1/4 cup
Yeast *fast rise*		
1 tsp.	1 1/2 tsp.	2 tsp.
- or -		
Yeast *active dry*		
2 tsp.	3 tsp.	4 tsp.

- To toast almonds, see page 52.

- Our Paskha recipe is on page 143.

Multi-Grain and More

Calories 171   Protein 14 %
Cholesterol 6 mg.   Carbohydrates 73 %
Sodium 318 mg.   Fat 16 %

Nutritional information per serving

We call this bread "Multi-Grain and More" because it's so packed with good-for-you stuff. All those grains give it a full, rich flavor – and enough body to stick to your ribs. If you want the benefits of cereal and the timeliness of toast, this is the bread for you.

Success Hints

- Any unsweetened multi-grain cereal should work in this bread.

- For accent and crunch, sprinkle a few oats on top after the final rise, just before baking.

- Try with Gruyere Apple Spread - page 143.

- This recipe can be made with the whole wheat, white, rapid, or delay bake cycles.

REGULAR	LARGE	EXTRA LARGE
Water		
3/4 cup	1 1/4 cups	1 1/2 cups
Butter		
1 Tbsp.	2 Tbsp.	2 Tbsp.
Honey		
1 1/2 Tbsp.	3 Tbsp.	4 Tbsp.
White Bread Flour		
1 1/4 cups	2 1/4 cups	2 1/2 cups
Whole Wheat Flour		
1/4 cup	1/2 cup	1/2 cup
Dry Milk		
1 Tbsp.	2 Tbsp.	2 Tbsp.
Salt		
1 tsp.	1 1/2 tsp.	2 tsp.
7 Grain Rolled Cereal		
1/4 cup	1/2 cup	1/2 cup
Wheat Germ		
2 Tbsp.	3 Tbsp.	1/4 cup
Oat Bran		
1 Tbsp.	2 Tbsp.	2 Tbsp.
Cracked Wheat		
1 Tbsp.	2 Tbsp.	2 Tbsp.
Yeast *fast rise*		
1 tsp.	2 tsp.	2 tsp.
- or -		
Yeast *active dry*		
1 1/2 tsp.	3 tsp.	3 tsp.

Honey Mustard

Calories 126
Cholesterol 0 mg.
Sodium 217 mg.

Protein 16 %
Carbohydrates 79 %
Fat 8 %

Nutritional information per serving

You don't need to love mustard to love this bread. The mustard adds a subtle, secondary flavor. This bread makes an unforgettable ham sandwich, or it can be served warm with baked ham or roast duck.

Success Hints

- We like Grey Poupon Country Dijon Mustard in this recipe.

- Experiment with your favorite mustard flavors.

- This recipe can be made with the white, rapid, or delay bake cycles.

REGULAR	LARGE	EXTRA LARGE
Water		
3/4 cup	1 1/3 cups	1 1/2 cups
Honey		
2 1/2 Tbsp.	1/4 cup	1/3 cup
Gourmet Mustard		
1 2/3 Tbsp.	3 Tbsp.	3 Tbsp.
White Bread Flour		
1 1/2 cups	2 cups	3 cups
Whole Wheat Flour		
1/2 cup	1 cup	1 cup
Dry Milk		
2 tsp.	1 Tbsp.	1 1/3 Tbsp.
Salt		
1/2 tsp.	1 tsp.	1 tsp.
Chives *dried*		
1 tsp.	1 Tbsp.	1 Tbsp.
Yeast *fast rise*		
1 tsp.	1 1/2 tsp.	1 1/2 tsp.
- or -		
Yeast *active dry*		
2 tsp.	2 tsp.	3 tsp.

Apple Oat

Calories 198 Protein 12 %
Cholesterol 4 mg. Carbohydrates 77 %
Sodium 297 mg. Fat 9 %

Nutritional information per serving

This is a full-bodied oatmeal bread with the added sweetness of apples and honey. It goes well with smoked meats such as summer sausage. For something different, try a curried turkey salad filling.

Success Hints

- Use unsweetened apples, canned in water. Drain well and chop into chunks.

- Use frozen apple juice concentrate, thawed, with no water added.

- If canned apples are not available, peel and chop fresh apples, microwave for 2 minutes, then drain before adding.

- This recipe can be made with the white or rapid bake cycles.

	REGULAR	LARGE	EXTRA LARGE
Water	1/2 cup	2/3 cup	3/4 cup
Butter	2 tsp.	1 1/2 Tbsp.	1 1/2 Tbsp.
Apples *canned/chopped*	1/2 cup	3/4 cup	1 cup
Apple Juice *concentrated*	1 Tbsp.	2 Tbsp.	2 Tbsp.
Lemon Juice	2 tsp.	1 Tbsp.	4 tsp.
Honey	1 Tbsp.	2 Tbsp.	2 Tbsp.
Yogurt *plain/nonfat*	2 Tbsp.	1/4 cup	1/4 cup
Molasses	2 tsp.	1 Tbsp.	4 tsp.
White Bread Flour	1 1/3 cups	2 cups	2 2/3 cups
Whole Wheat Flour	2/3 cup	1 cup	1 1/3 cups
Dry Milk	2 tsp.	1 Tbsp.	4 tsp.
Salt	1 tsp.	1 1/2 tsp.	2 tsp.
Oats	1/4 cup	1/2 cup	1/2 cup
Yeast *fast rise*	1 tsp.	1 tsp.	1 1/2 tsp.
- or -			
Yeast *active dry*	2 tsp.	2 tsp.	3 tsp.

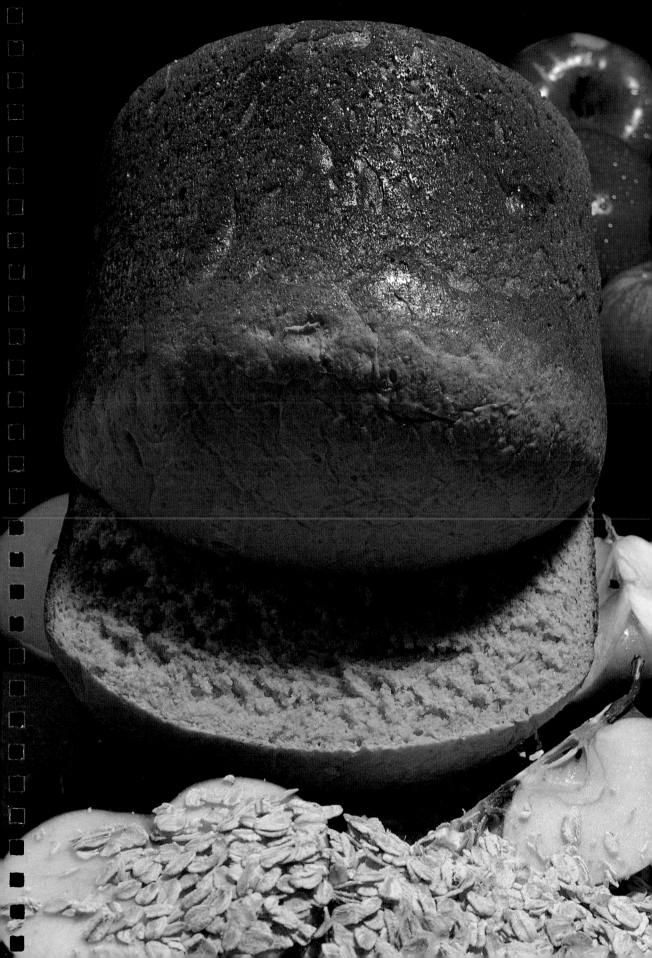

Peanut Butter

Calories 203   Protein 14 %
Cholesterol 0 mg.   Carbohydrates 61 %
Sodium 273 mg.   Fat 26 %

Nutritional information per serving

Jim, our unofficial humorist, says, "At last, a peanut butter that doesn't stick to the roof of your mouth!" Top with honey or jam for a peanut butter sandwich in half the time. Although kids devour it, don't forget to share the fun and flavor with a few grown ups, too.

REGULAR	LARGE	EXTRA LARGE
Water		
3/4 cup	1 1/4 cups	1 1/2 cups
Peanut Butter		
1/3 cup	1/2 cup	2/3 cup
White Bread Flour		
2 cups	3 cups	4 cups
Brown Sugar		
2 1/2 Tbsp.	1/4 cup	5 Tbsp.
Salt		
1/4 tsp.	1 1/2 tsp.	2 tsp.
Yeast *fast rise*		
1 tsp.	1 1/2 tsp.	1 1/2 tsp.
- *or* -		
Yeast *active dry*		
2 tsp.	3 tsp.	3 1/2 tsp.

Success Hints

- Use your choice of creamy or crunchy quality peanut butter.

- Fill with jam and cut into fun shapes for pre-school luncheon or children's party.

- This recipe can be made with the white, rapid, or delay bake cycles.

Certainly Citrus

Calories 168	**Protein 12 %**	
Cholesterol 4 mg.	**Carbohydrates 76 %**	
Sodium 298 mg.	**Fat 13 %**	

Nutritional information per serving

This tangy bread has a fine, light texture. The subtle yet distinctive flavor makes it a perfect accompaniment for fish or chicken. Try it with swordfish baked with lime butter or your favorite lemon chicken recipe.

Success Hints

- If using fresh lemon peel, zest very fine and avoid using the white pulp.

- This is a moist dough and the crust on this bread is a naturally light color.

- Try this bread with the Cheesy Lemon spread - page 143.

- This recipe can be made with the white, sweet or rapid bake cycles.

REGULAR	LARGE	EXTRA LARGE
Water		
5/8 cup	7/8 cup	1 1/8 cups
Butter		
1 Tbsp.	1 1/2 Tbsp.	1 1/2 Tbsp.
Orange Marmalade		
1/4 cup	1/3 cup	1/2 cup
Lemon Juice		
2 tsp.	1 Tbsp.	1 1/2 Tbsp.
Lime Juice		
2 tsp.	1 Tbsp.	1 1/2 Tbsp.
White Bread Flour		
2 cups	3 cups	4 cups
Dry Milk		
1 Tbsp.	2 Tbsp.	2 Tbsp.
Salt		
1 tsp.	1 1/2 tsp.	2 tsp.
Lemon Peel		
1/8 tsp.	1/8 tsp.	1/4 tsp.
Yeast *fast rise*		
1 tsp.	1 1/2 tsp.	1 1/2 tsp.
- or -		
Yeast *active dry*		
1 1/2 tsp.	2 tsp.	2 1/2 tsp.

Cottage Dill

Calories 166
Cholesterol 5 mg.
Sodium 350 mg.

Protein 17 %
Carbohydrates 70 %
Fat 14 %

Nutritional information per serving

This bread will make a bread machine believer out of anyone. The aroma is heaven, and the taste lives up to the aroma. Cottage Dill is best served warm from the oven or toaster; the heat liberates the spices for a full, rich flavor.

Success Hints

- Use small curd, low fat cottage cheese.

- The liquid in cottage cheese varies. If your dough is too dry, try adding water a tablespoon at a time during the kneading until dough appears moist and pliable and forms a ball.

- This recipe can be made with the white or rapid bake cycles.

REGULAR	LARGE	EXTRA LARGE
Water		
1/2 cup	3/4 cup	1 cup
Butter		
1 Tbsp.	1 1/2 Tbsp.	2 Tbsp.
Cottage Cheese		
1/4 cup	3/4 cup	1/2 cup
White Bread Flour		
2 cups	3 cups	4 cups
Dry Milk		
1 Tbsp.	1 1/2 Tbsp.	2 Tbsp.
Sugar		
1 Tbsp.	2 Tbsp.	2 Tbsp.
Salt		
1 tsp.	1 1/2 tsp.	2 tsp.
Dry Onion		
1 1/2 tsp.	1 Tbsp.	1 Tbsp.
Dill Seed		
1 1/2 tsp.	1 Tbsp.	1 Tbsp.
Dill Weed		
1 tsp.	1 1/2 tsp.	2 tsp.
Yeast *fast rise*		
1 tsp.	1 1/2 tsp.	1 1/2 tsp.
- or -		
Yeast *active dry*		
2 tsp.	2 tsp.	1 Tbsp.

Cajun Spice

Calories 164   Protein 15 %
Cholesterol 6 mg.   Carbohydrates 71 %
Sodium 217 mg.   Fat 16 %

Nutritional information per serving

This is not a shy little bread to quench the fire of jambalaya or your blackened redfish. This is a bread with legs, bread that will get up and dance to Zydeco music all by itself! The Cajun spice mix promises to send a wake-up call to your taste buds when you serve it with salad or red beans and rice.

Success Hints

- Paul Prudhomme's Seafood Magic Spice is a great Cajun blend to use.

- Morton and Bassett makes a tasty salt-free Cajun blend. If using a no-salt blend, double the amount of the spice mix in the recipe.

- If using other spice blends, you may need to adjust the spice and salt amounts.

- This recipe can be made with the white or rapid bake cycle

REGULAR	LARGE	EXTRA LARGE
Water		
3/4 cup	1 cup	1 1/4 cups
Butter		
1 Tbsp.	2 Tbsp.	2 Tbsp.
Tomato Paste		
2 tsp.	2 Tbsp.	2 Tbsp.
White Bread Flour		
2 cups	3 cups	3 1/2 cups
Dry Milk		
1 Tbsp.	2 Tbsp.	2 Tbsp.
Brown Sugar		
1 Tbsp.	1 1/2 Tbsp.	2 Tbsp.
Salt		
1/2 tsp.	1 tsp.	1 tsp.
Onion Powder		
1/4 tsp.	1/2 tsp.	1/2 tsp.
Cajun Spice Blend		
1 Tbsp.	1 1/2 Tbsp.	2 Tbsp.
Parsley Flakes		
1/4 tsp.	1 tsp.	1 1/2 tsp.
Yeast *fast rise*		
1 1/4 tsp.	1 1/2 tsp.	1 1/2 tsp.
- or -		
Yeast *active dry*		
2 tsp.	2 1/2 tsp.	2 1/2 tsp.

Almond Poppy

Calories 196
Cholesterol 5 mg.
Sodium 203 mg.

Protein 14 %
Carbohydrates 63 %
Fat 27 %

Nutritional information per serving

This soft yellow bread is reminiscent of your favorite poppy seed muffin, but versatile enough to take you from breakfast to dessert. Start the day enjoying it with a touch of sweet butter on a freshly toasted slice. Savor with tea in the afternoon. After dinner, celebrate this winning dessert bread by topping slices with our Cheesy Lemon spread. Mmmmm.

Success Hints

- Toast almonds lightly in a shallow pan. *Stirring frequently,* bake at 350° for five minutes or until golden brown.

- For a luscious dessert bread, serve with the Cheesy Lemon spread - page 143.

- This recipe can be made with the white or rapid bake cycles.

REGULAR	LARGE	EXTRA LARGE
Water		
1/2 cup	3/4 cup	1 cup
Butter		
1 Tbsp.	1 1/2 Tbsp.	2 Tbsp.
Lemon Yogurt		
1/4 cup	1/2 cup	1/2 cup
Honey		
1 1/2 Tbsp.	2 Tbsp.	3 Tbsp.
Lemon Extract		
1 tsp.	2 tsp.	2 tsp.
White Bread Flour		
2 cups	3 cups	4 cups
Dry Milk		
1 Tbsp.	1 1/2 Tbsp.	2 Tbsp.
Salt		
1 tsp.	1 tsp.	2 tsp.
Almonds *sliced & toasted*		
1/4 cup	1/2 cup	3/4 cup
Lemon Peel *dried*		
2 tsp.	1 Tbsp.	1 1/2 Tbsp.
Poppy Seeds		
2 Tbsp.	3 Tbsp.	1/4 cup
Yeast *fast rise*		
1 tsp.	1 1/2 tsp.	1 1/2 tsp.
- or -		
Yeast *active dry*		
2 tsp.	2 tsp.	3 tsp.

Honey Wheat

Calories 153   Protein 13 %
Cholesterol 6 mg.   Carbohydrates 73 %
Sodium 297 mg.   Fat 16 %
Nutritional information per serving

REGULAR	LARGE	EXTRA LARGE
Water		
3/4 cup	1 cup	1 1/4 cups
Honey		
1 Tbsp.	1 1/2 Tbsp.	2 Tbsp.
Butter		
1 Tbsp.	2 Tbsp.	2 Tbsp.
White Bread Flour		
1 1/2 cups	2 1/2 cups	3 cups
Whole Wheat Flour		
1/2 cup	1/2 cup	1 cup
Dry Milk		
1 Tbsp.	1 1/2 Tbsp.	2 Tbsp.
Salt		
1 tsp.	1 1/2 tsp.	2 tsp.
Yeast *fast rise*		
1 tsp.	1 1/2 tsp.	1 1/2 tsp.
- or -		
Yeast *active dry*		
1 1/2 tsp.	1 1/2 tsp.	1 1/2 tsp.

Want to know how far you can go with this bread? Our friend, Ed Rasmuson, even takes his bread machine hunting! The first year Ed took his home bakery on his annual trek to Kodiak, he caught some razzing. But eight days and eight loaves later, his buddies were hooked. "They all kind of laughed when I bought my bread machine," Ed reports, "but they don't laugh anymore." A basic whole wheat like this is one of the group's favorites.

Success Hints

- Just follow the recipe, use a good bread flour, and you can't go wrong.

- Try this bread with our Honey Butter - page 143.

- This recipe can be made with the white, rapid, or delay bake cycles.

Garlic

Calories 163   Protein 12 %
Cholesterol 1 mg.   Carbohydrates 67 %
Sodium 295 mg.   Fat 19 %

Nutritional information per serving

When Lynn put her house on the market, we offered this advice: "If you want to sell your house, bake garlic bread when people are coming through!" The aroma of this bread is to die for - and it butters up to make the easiest garlic toast around.

Success Hints

- For a fresher taste, grate your own fresh parmesan cheese.

- Serve this bread warm. The flavor is definitely enhanced.

- Garlic paste may be substituted for minced garlic.

- For a milder flavor, omit the chives and black pepper.

- This recipe can be made with the white, rapid or delay bake cycles.

REGULAR	LARGE	EXTRA LARGE
Water		
3/4 cup	1 1/8 cups	1 3/8 cups
Olive Oil		
1 Tbsp.	2 Tbsp.	3 Tbsp.
Garlic *finely minced*		
1/2 tsp.	3/4 tsp.	1 tsp.
White Bread Flour		
2 cups	3 cups	4 cups
Sugar		
1 Tbsp.	2 Tbsp.	3 Tbsp.
Salt		
1 tsp.	1 1/2 tsp.	2 tsp.
Parmesan *grated*		
2 Tbsp.	3 Tbsp.	1/4 cup
Sweet Basil		
1/2 tsp.	3/4 tsp.	1 tsp.
Garlic Powder		
1/2 tsp.	3/4 tsp.	1 tsp.
Chives *dried/chopped*		
1 Tbsp.	2 Tbsp.	3 Tbsp.
Black Pepper *course ground*		
1/2 tsp.	3/4 tsp.	1 tsp.
Yeast *fast rise*		
1 tsp.	2 tsp.	2 1/2 tsp.
- or -		
Yeast *active dry*		
1 1/2 tsp.	2 tsp.	3 tsp.

Saffron

Calories 156
Cholesterol 18 mg.
Sodium 276 mg.

Protein 13 %
Carbohydrates 67 %
Fat 17 %

Nutritional information per serving

Saffron is the world's most expensive spice - 225,000 crocus stigmas are needed to make a single pound! The texture and flavor of this light and fluffy loaf will convince you it's worth it. This is bread for a special occasion - or bread that will make any occasion special. The distinctive Old World flavor works magic with seafood and hearty soups like lentil or sausage.

Success Hints

- Break egg into liquid measuring cup, then fill with water to the combined egg and water measurement.

- If using Saffron thread, grind to a coarse powder-like consistency using a mortar and pestle.

- Once opened, the intensity of a vial of saffron will diminish.

- This recipe can be made with the white or rapid bake cycles.

REGULAR	LARGE	EXTRA LARGE
1 Egg plus Water to equal		
3/4 cup	1 1/4 cups	1 1/2 cups
Olive Oil		
1 1/2 Tbsp.	2 Tbsp.	3 Tbsp.
White Bread Flour		
2 cups	3 cups	4 cups
Sugar		
1 tsp.	1 1/2 tsp.	1 Tbsp.
Salt		
1 tsp.	1 1/2 tsp.	2 tsp.
Saffron *ground*		
1/4 tsp.	1/2 tsp.	1/2 tsp.
- or -		
Saffron *threads*		
1/8 tsp.	1/4 tsp.	1/4 tsp.
Yeast *fast rise*		
1 tsp.	1 1/2 tsp.	1 1/2 tsp.
- or -		
Yeast *active dry*		
2 tsp.	2 tsp.	2 tsp.

Maraschino Pecan

Calories 196　　　Protein 14 %
Cholesterol 3 mg.　Carbohydrates 67 %
Sodium 244 mg.　　Fat 27 %

Nutritional information per serving

You can dress this bread up or down, and you'll love it either way. Combine green and red maraschino cherries for a festive holiday bread, or substitute your favorite dried fruits for a sweet morning meal with a light crunch. The pecans offer a perfect counterpart to the fruit.

Success Hints

- Drain cherries well on a paper towel.

- Add cherries whole for appearance.

- Add the fruit and nuts at the beep on the fruit and nut cycle or at the end of the first knead.

- Try replacing half the cherries with chopped dried apricots, pears, dates or apples.

- This recipe can be made with the white, rapid, sweet or delay bake cycles.

REGULAR	LARGE	EXTRA LARGE
Water		
3/4 cup	1 cup	1 1/3 cups
Butter		
2 tsp.	1 Tbsp.	1 Tbsp.
Maraschino Cherries		
7 each	9 each	11 each
White Bread Flour		
2 cups	3 cups	4 cups
Dry Milk		
1 Tbsp.	1 1/2 Tbsp.	2 Tbsp.
Sugar		
4 tsp.	2 Tbsp.	2 Tbsp.
Salt		
3/4 tsp.	1 1/4 tsp.	1 1/4 tsp.
Raisins		
2 1/2 Tbsp.	1/4 cup	1/4 cup
Sunflower Seeds		
2 1/2 Tbsp.	1/4 cup	1/4 cup
Pecans *chopped*		
2 1/2 Tbsp.	1/4 cup	1/4 cup
Ground Cinnamon		
1/8 tsp.	1/4 tsp.	1/2 tsp.
Ground Ginger		
1/8 tsp.	1/4 tsp.	1/4 tsp.
Yeast *fast rise*		
1 1/2 tsp.	1 tsp.	1 1/2 tsp.
- or -		
Yeast *active dry*		
2 tsp.	2 tsp.	2 tsp.

Easy French

Calories 134	Protein 12 %
Cholesterol 0 mg.	Carbohydrates 80 %
Sodium 271 mg.	Fat 4 %

Nutritional information per serving

REGULAR	LARGE	EXTRA LARGE
Water		
3/4 cup	1 1/4 cups	1 1/2 cups
White Bread Flour		
2 cups	3 cups	4 cups
Sugar		
1 1/4 Tbsp.	1 1/2 Tbsp.	2 1/2 Tbsp.
Salt		
1 tsp.	1 1/2 tsp.	2 tsp.
Yeast *fast rise*		
3/4 tsp.	2 tsp.	1 1/2 tsp.
- or -		
Yeast *active dry*		
1 1/4 tsp.	3 tsp.	2 1/2 tsp.

Our Easy French is exactly that – *easy*. It may look a little different, but from its crusty crust to its light, chewy interior, it tastes great. This recipe was created for machines without a French bread baking cycle: it mixes, rises and bakes entirely in your machine. Or you can make a traditional loaf from this recipe using our Picnic Basket process instructions on page 138.

Success Hints

- When the bread comes out of the machine, the crust color may look light to you. This is normal for this loaf.

- This recipe can be used with white, French, rapid and delay bake cycles.

Light Rye

Calories 145   Protein 11 %
Cholesterol 4 mg.   Carbohydrates 74 %
Sodium 240 mg.   Fat 12 %

Nutritional information per serving

In the mood for your favorite ham and cheese sandwich? This is the bread for you. This light loaf was created with sandwiches in mind. Slice it, fill it, and let your tastebuds take it from there.

Success Hints

- ■ . Just follow the recipe. It's that easy!

- ■ This recipe can be made with the white, rapid, or delay bake cycles.

	REGULAR	LARGE	EXTRA LARGE
Water	3/4 cup	1 1/8 cups	1 1/2 cups
Butter	1 Tbsp.	4 tsp.	4 1/2 tsp.
White Bread Flour	1 1/2 cups	2 1/4 cups	3 cups
Rye Flour	1/2 cup	3/4 cup	1 cup
Sugar	1 1/2 Tbsp.	2 1/2 Tbsp.	3 Tbsp.
Salt	3/4 tsp.	1 1/4 tsp.	1 1/2 tsp.
Cornmeal	2 tsp.	1 Tbsp.	4 tsp.
Caraway Seeds	1 tsp.	1 1/2 tsp.	2 tsp.
Yeast *fast rise*	1 1/4 tsp.	2 tsp.	2 1/2 tsp.
- or -			
Yeast *active dry*	2 tsp.	3 tsp.	4 tsp.

Sweet Coconut Curry

Calories 190   Protein 13 %
Cholesterol 6 mg.   Carbohydrates 72 %
Sodium 309 mg.   Fat 18 %

Nutritional information per serving

Colorful and unexpected, this bread is as distinctive as the country that inspired it. The raisins and coconut lend a slight sweetness, but the flavor and aroma are distinctly curry. Serve it with your favorite rice and meat dish.

Success Hints

- If you like more kick in your curry, use hot curry.

- Believe it or not, this bread is really good spread with peanut butter.

- This recipe can be made with the white, rapid, or delay bake cycles.

REGULAR	LARGE	EXTRA LARGE
Water		
3/4 cup	1 1/4 cups	1 1/2 cups
Butter		
1 Tbsp.	2 Tbsp.	2 Tbsp.
White Bread Flour		
2 cups	3 cups	4 cups
Dry Milk		
1Tbsp.	2 Tbsp.	2 Tbsp.
Brown Sugar		
1 Tbsp.	2 Tbsp.	2 Tbsp.
Salt		
1 tsp.	1 1/2 tsp.	2 tsp.
Raisins		
1/3 cup	1/2 cup	2/3 cup
Coconut Flakes		
1/3 cup	1/2 cup	2/3 cup
Curry Powder		
2 tsp.	1 Tbsp.	1 1/3 tsp.
Yeast *fast rise*		
1 1/2 tsp.	2 tsp.	2 1/2 tsp.
- or -		
Yeast *active dry*		
2 tsp.	3 tsp.	3 1/2 tsp.

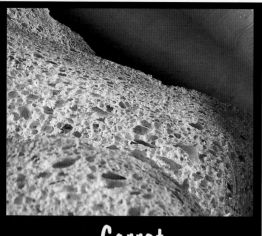

Carrot

Calories 175
Cholesterol 0 mg.
Sodium 283 mg.

Protein 14 %
Carbohydrates 78 %
Fat 10 %

Nutritional information per serving

Getting your beta carotene was never this easy - or this tasty. The wheat flour gives this bread body, the nuts and carrots give it texture, and the yogurt keeps it moist. Serve this bread with steaming bowls of vegetable soup for a nutritious, hearty lunch.

Success Hints

- Use freshly grated carrots.

- This recipe is best made with the white bake cycle.

REGULAR	LARGE	EXTRA LARGE
Water		
1/2 cup	3/4 cup	1 cup
Yogurt *plain*		
2 Tbsp.	1/4 cup	1/4 cup
Carrots *grated*		
2/3 cup	1 cup	1 1/3 cups
Honey		
1 Tbsp.	2 Tbsp.	2 Tbsp.
Molasses		
1 Tbsp.	2 Tbsp.	2 Tbsp.
White Bread Flour		
1 1/3 cups	2 1/4 cups	2 2/3 cups
Whole Wheat Flour		
2/3 cup	1 cup	1 1/3 cups
Dry Milk		
2 tsp.	1 Tbsp.	4 tsp.
Salt		
1 tsp.	1 1/2 tsp.	2 tsp.
Walnuts *chopped*		
2 Tbsp.	1/4 cup	1/4 cup
Yeast *fast rise*		
1 tsp.	1 1/2 tsp.	1 1/2 tsp.
- or -		
Yeast *active dry*		
2 tsp.	2 tsp.	2 tsp.

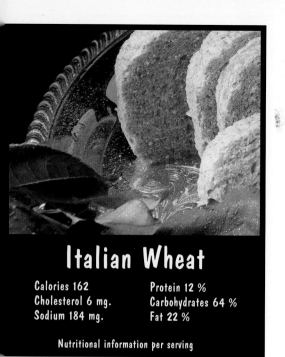

Italian Wheat

Calories 162   Protein 12 %
Cholesterol 6 mg.   Carbohydrates 64 %
Sodium 184 mg.   Fat 22 %

Nutritional information per serving

The combination of easy preparation and fabulous flavor create a
bread that makes a terrific impres-
sion without much work. This is a
light wheat bread with a succulent
pesto flavor. Serve it plain or use it
for garlic bread with spaghetti or
lasagna.

Success Hints

- Use a freshly prepared pesto sauce
  or make your own. Stir the sauce
  well before measuring to blend oil.

- Make a quick slice of pizza by topping with marinara sauce and cheese,
  then toast under the broiler.

- This recipe can be made with the
  white, rapid or delay bake cycles.

REGULAR	LARGE	EXTRA LARGE
Water		
2/3 cup	1 cup	1 1/4 cups
Butter		
4 tsp.	2 Tbsp.	2 1/2 Tbsp.
White Bread Flour		
1 1/2 cups	2 cups	3 cups
Whole Wheat Flour		
1/2 cup	1 cup	1 cup
Sugar		
1 Tbsp.	1 1/2 Tbsp.	2 Tbsp.
Salt		
1/2 tsp.	3/4 tsp.	1 tsp.
Pesto Sauce		
1/4 cup	1/4 cup	1/3 cup
Yeast *fast rise*		
1 tsp.	1 tsp.	1 tsp.
- or - **Yeast** *active dry*		
1 1/2 tsp.	2 tsp.	2 tsp.

Bits o' Bacon

Calories 165　　　　Protein 15 %
Cholesterol 8 mg.　　Carbohydrates 65 %
Sodium 354 mg.　　　Fat 22 %

Nutritional information per serving

The preparations for this bread may be a little more complex than most, but don't be put off – the finished product is definitely worth it. This is one of those loaves the whole family eats up, right out of the oven. If it lasts long enough, this tasty loaf enlivens any soup or salad.

Success Hints

■ Cook bacon until almost crisp. Set bacon fat aside while you crumble cooked bacon, then remix bacon and fat before measuring.

■ Extra pepper may be added to taste.

■ After loaf is partially cooled, brush with butter and sprinkle a little coarsely ground salt on top.

■ This recipe can be made with the white or rapid bake cycles.

REGULAR	LARGE	EXTRA LARGE
Water		
2/3 cup	1 cup	1 1/3 cups
Butter		
4 tsp.	2 Tbsp.	3 Tbsp.
Bacon *with fat*		
1/4 cup	1/3 cup	1/2 cup
White Bread Flour		
1 2/3 cups	2 1/2 cups	3 1/3 cups
Whole Wheat Flour		
1/3 cup	1/2 cup	2/3 cup
Sugar		
4 tsp.	2 Tbsp.	3 Tbsp.
Salt		
1 tsp.	1 1/2 tsp.	2 tsp.
Green Peppercorns *dried/crushed*		
1/2 tsp.	3/4 tsp.	1 tsp.
Sweet Basil *dried*		
1/2 tsp.	3/4 tsp.	1 tsp.
Garlic Powder		
pinch	1/4 tsp.	1/4 tsp.
Yeast *fast rise*		
1 tsp.	1 1/2 tsp.	2 tsp.
- or -		
Yeast *active dry*		
2 tsp.	2 1/2 tsp.	4 tsp.

Saucy Apple

Calories 181
Cholesterol 0 mg.
Sodium 277 mg.

Protein 11 %
Carbohydrates 77 %
Fat 14 %

Nutritional information per serving

REGULAR	LARGE	EXTRA LARGE
Apple Cider		
2/3 cup	7/8 cup	1 1/4 cups
Applesauce *unsweetened*		
1/4 cup	1/3 cup	1/2 cup
Granny Smith Apple *chopped/unpeeled*		
1/3 cup	1/2 cup	2/3 cup
White Bread Flour		
1 1/2 cups	2 1/4 cups	3 cups
Whole Wheat Flour		
1/2 cup	3/4 cup	1 cup
Salt		
1 tsp.	1 1/2 tsp.	2 tsp.
Walnuts *unchopped*		
1/4 cup	1/3 cup	1/2 cup
Instant Apple Cider *powdered mix*		
2 Tbsp.	3 1/2 Tbsp.	1/4 cup
Yeast *fast rise*		
1 tsp.	1 1/2 tsp.	2 tsp.
- or -		
Yeast *active dry*		
1 1/2 tsp.	2 tsp.	2 1/2 tsp.

Did you ever hear the cooking tip about putting a slice of fresh apple in your cake saver to keep your cake moist? Well, the fresh Granny Smith apple in this recipe works the same way in this tangy, long-lasting bread. Even days later, it retains a nice moistness that makes it a favorite for those times when you need to bake ahead.

Success Hints

- Instant apple cider mix is found next to teas and other hot beverages in the grocery store.

- Core and dice unpeeled apple.

- The Granny Smith apple adds tartness. For a sweeter bread, try using a Rome or a McIntosh apple, and replacing apple cider with apple juice.

- This recipe can be made with the white or rapid bake cycles.

Baked Potato

Calories 163
Cholesterol 5 mg.
Sodium 327 mg.

Protein 15 %
Carbohydrates 71 %
Fat 17 %

Nutritional information per serving

If you are a meat and potatoes kind of person, this is the bread for you. Just add butter, and you have a potato loaf with all the trimmings! The velvety texture and rich flavor make this bread a wonderful companion to roasts, and a natural for meatloaf sandwiches. Served warm, it turns a bowl of vegetable beef soup into a memorable meal.

Success Hints

- This dough will be very dry. Resist the urge to add water.

- For best flavor, use real bacon bits.

- For a taste treat, top with our Jezebel Jam - page 142.

- This recipe can be baked with the white or rapid bake cycles.

REGULAR	LARGE	EXTRA LARGE
Water		
1/2 cup	3/4 cup	1 cup
Sour Cream		
1/4 cup	1/2 cup	1/2 cup
Bacon Bits		
1 1/2 Tbsp.	3 Tbsp.	1/4 cup
White Bread Flour		
2 cups	3 cups	4 cups
Dry Milk		
1 Tbsp.	1 1/2 Tbsp.	2 Tbsp.
Sugar		
1 Tbsp.	1 1/2 Tbsp.	2 Tbsp.
Salt		
1 tsp.	1 1/2 tsp.	2 tsp.
Potato Flakes *instant*		
1 1/2 Tbsp.	3 Tbsp.	1/4 cup
Chives *dried*		
1 1/2 Tbsp.	3 Tbsp.	1/4 cup
Yeast *fast rise*		
1 tsp.	2 tsp.	2 tsp.
- or - **Yeast** *active dry*		
2 tsp.	3 tsp.	3 tsp.

100% Crunch

Calories 197	Protein 12 %	
Cholesterol 0 mg.	Carbohydrates 63 %	
Sodium 274 mg.	Fat 32 %	

Nutritional information per serving

We created this bread for people who think 100% whole wheat is boring. The seeds inject a crunchy, chewy texture so satisfying, you won't even need a toaster for crispness. High in fiber and high in taste, 100% Crunch brings a new dimension to an avocado and sprout sandwich.

Success Hints

- We used equal amounts of pumpkin seeds, flax seeds and sunflower seeds.

- Try using different seeds or chopped nuts for different taste and texture. (No bird seed, please!)

- Gluten is available in health food stores and nutritional departments.

- This recipe can be made with the whole wheat, white or delay bake cycles.

REGULAR	LARGE	EXTRA LARGE
Water		
3/4 cup	1 1/4 cup	1 1/2 cups
Honey		
4 tsp.	2 Tbsp.	2 Tbsp.
Molasses		
4 tsp.	2 Tbsp.	2 Tbsp.
Olive Oil		
4 tsp.	2 Tbsp.	2 Tbsp.
Whole Wheat Flour		
2 cups	3 cups	4 cups
Gluten		
2 tsp.	1 Tbsp.	1 Tbsp.
Salt		
1 tsp.	1 1/2 tsp.	2 tsp.
Seeds		
1/2 cup	2/3 cup	1 cup
Yeast *fast rise*		
1 tsp.	2 tsp.	2 tsp.
- or -		
Yeast *active dry*		
2 tsp.	3 tsp.	3 tsp.

Garden Herb

Calories 159   Protein 13 %
Cholesterol 6 mg.   Carbohydrates 65 %
Sodium 299 mg.   Fat 17 %

Nutritional information per serving

The fragrance of turkey stuffing will fill your home while this flavorful bread is baking, thanks to all those aromatic dried herbs. This loaf is excellent for any cold meat sandwich you can dream up – including turkey and cranberry – and it makes down-right tasty croutons.

Success Hints

- Use dried herbs that are flaked and not ground. If using fresh herbs, double the amount.

- To make Rosemary Bread, use half as much marjoram and thyme and replace the chives and the basil with *fresh* chopped rosemary.

- Any combination of spices may be substituted, according to your tastes.

- This recipe can be made with the white, rapid, or delay bake cycles.

	REGULAR	LARGE	EXTRA LARGE
Water	3/4 cup	1 1/4 cups	1 1/2 cups
Butter	1 Tbsp.	2 Tbsp.	2 Tbsp.
White Bread Flour	2 cups	3 cups	4 cups
Dry Milk	1 Tbsp.	2 Tbsp.	2 Tbsp.
Sugar	1 Tbsp.	2 Tbsp.	2 Tbsp.
Salt	1 tsp.	1 1/2 tsp.	2 tsp.
Chives	1 tsp.	2 tsp.	1 Tbsp.
Marjoram	1 tsp.	2 tsp.	1 Tbsp.
Thyme	1 tsp.	2 tsp.	1 Tbsp.
Basil	1/2 tsp.	1 tsp.	1 tsp.
Yeast *fast rise*	1 tsp.	1 1/2 tsp.	1 1/2 tsp.
- or - **Yeast** *active dry*	2 tsp.	2 tsp.	2 tsp.

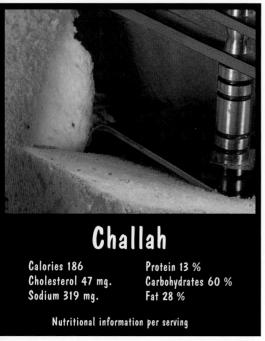

Challah

Calories 186
Cholesterol 47 mg.
Sodium 319 mg.

Protein 13 %
Carbohydrates 60 %
Fat 28 %

Nutritional information per serving

	REGULAR	LARGE	EXTRA LARGE
1 Egg plus Water to equal	3/4 cup	1 cup	1 1/4 cups
Butter	2 1/2 Tbsp.	1/4 cup	1/4 cup
Egg Yolk	1	1	2
White Bread Flour	2 cups	3 cups	4 cups
Sugar	1 Tbsp.	2 Tbsp.	2 Tbsp.
Salt	1 tsp.	1 1/2 tsp.	2 tsp.
Poppy Seeds	1/2 tsp.	3/4 tsp.	1 tsp.
Yeast *fast rise*	3/4 tsp.	1 tsp.	1 tsp.
- or - **Yeast** *active dry*	1 1/2 tsp.	2 tsp.	3 tsp.

This light egg bread represents the manna of the desert in Jewish tradition. Like many busy people, Rabbi Harry Rosenfeld of Anchorage's Temple Beth Sholom makes his Sabbath Challah in his home bread machine. "I use it the way it comes out of the machine," he says. "It tastes fine. We use it regularly." For special holidays, the dough can be styled into a variety of shapes.

Success Hints

- Break egg into liquid measuring cup, then fill with water to the combined egg and water measurement.

- The egg content of this bread makes it a perfect base for a nice rich stuffing.

- This recipe may be baked on the white or rapid bake cycles.

- For traditional braided Challah, mix ingredients (without poppy seeds) in the dough cycle. Then follow the process steps for Saffron Braids on page 128. Brush with beaten egg and top with poppy seeds. Lift onto greased baking sheet and allow to double, about one hour. Bake at 375° for 20-25 minutes.

Mocha Java

Calories 186	Protein 13 %
Cholesterol 24 mg.	Carbohydrates 58 %
Sodium 305 mg.	Fat 33 %

Nutritional information per serving

This is a coffee lover's bread. It goes great with a cup of rich French Roast any time of day, making any coffee break feel like a brunch. Serve it with a light spread of cream cheese for an even richer flavor.

Success Hints

■ Break egg into liquid measuring cup, then fill with water to the combined egg and water measurement.

■ Try your favorite instant coffee mixes, such as Cappuccino or Vienna. Use sugar-free mixes.

■ For an alternative, use sugar-free cocoa mix instead of the coffee mix.

■ This recipe can be made with white or rapid bake cycles.

REGULAR	LARGE	EXTRA LARGE
1 Egg plus Water to equal		
3/4 cup	1 1/4 cups	1 1/2 cups
Butter		
1 1/2 Tbsp.	2 Tbsp.	3 Tbsp.
White Bread Flour		
1 3/4 cups	2 1/3 cups	3 1/2 cups
Dry Milk		
1 Tbsp.	2 Tbsp.	2 Tbsp.
Rye Flour		
1/4 cup	1/2 cup	1/2 cup
Salt		
1 tsp.	1 1/2 tsp.	2 tsp.
Brown Sugar		
1 1/2 Tbsp.	3 Tbsp.	1/4 cup
Instant Mocha *sugarfree coffee mix*		
1 Tbsp.	2 Tbsp.	2 Tbsp.
Pecans *chopped*		
1/4 cup	1/2 cup	1/2 cup
Yeast *fast rise*		
1 tsp.	1 1/2 tsp.	1 1/2 tsp.
- or -		
Yeast *active dry*		
2 tsp.	2 1/2 tsp.	2 1/2 tsp.

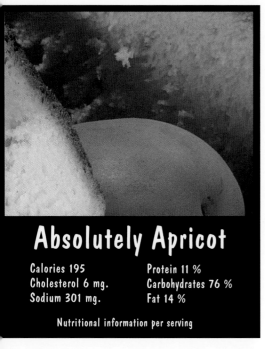

Absolutely Apricot

Calories 195   Protein 11 %
Cholesterol 6 mg.   Carbohydrates 76 %
Sodium 301 mg.   Fat 14 %

Nutritional information per serving

	REGULAR	LARGE	EXTRA LARGE
Water	3/4 cup	1 1/4 cup	1 1/2 cups
Butter	1 Tbsp.	2 Tbsp.	2 Tbsp.
Apricot Jam	3 Tbsp.	1/4 cup	1/4 cup
White Bread Flour	2 cups	3 cups	4 cups
Dry Milk	1 Tbsp.	2 Tbsp.	2 Tbsp.
Salt	1 tsp.	1 1/2 tsp.	2 tsp.
Dried Apricots *chopped*	1/2 cup	3/4 cup	1 cup
Yeast *fast rise*	1 tsp.	1 1/2 tsp.	1 1/2 tsp.
- or - **Yeast** *active dry*	2 tsp.	3 tsp.	3 tsp.

This is bread with the jam already inside. It's a coffee bread, a snack bread or the perfect after-school bread. This finely textured sweet bread also happens to be lovely, with the summery orange apricots floating in the golden loaf.

Success Hints

- Crust may brown more because of the sugar. If your machine offers the option, use the "light" crust feature.

- We use dried apricots preserved without sulfur dioxide. This preservative sometimes de-activates the yeast.

- Use a jam with a high fruit content and few other additives.

- This recipe can be baked with the white, rapid, or delay bake cycles.

Pumpernickel

Calories 159   **Protein** 12 %
Cholesterol 5 mg.   **Carbohydrates** 73 %
Sodium 297 mg.   **Fat** 17 %

Nutritional information per serving

This heavy, dark bread is a traditional pumpernickel - the kind that will leave you reaching for smoked salmon and cream cheese. The loaf is shorter and denser than most because of the heavy flours, but this fresh rich loaf could be the best pumpernickel you'll ever eat!

Success Hints

- It's not unusual for the top to be slightly honey-combed.

- This recipe is best made on the whole wheat cycle, but can also be made on the white or delay bake cycles.

	REGULAR	LARGE	EXTRA LARGE
Water	3/4 cup	1 1/4 cups	1 1/2 cups
Butter	1 Tbsp.	2 Tbsp.	2 Tbsp.
Molasses	3 Tbsp.	1/4 cup	1/3 cup
White Bread Flour	1 cup	1 1/2 cups	2 cups
Whole Wheat Flour	1/3 cup	1/2 cup	2/3 cup
Rye Flour	2/3 cup	1 cup	1 1/3 cups
Dry Milk	1 Tbsp.	4 tsp.	2 Tbsp.
Sugar	1 Tbsp.	2 Tbsp.	3 Tbsp.
Salt	1 tsp.	1 1/2 tsp.	2 tsp.
Cornmeal	2 Tbsp.	1/4 cup	1/4 cup
Cocoa *powdered*	2 Tbsp.	3 Tbsp.	1/4 cup
Instant Coffee	1/4 tsp.	1/2 tsp.	1/2 tsp.
Caraway Seeds	1 tsp.	2 tsp.	2 tsp.
Yeast *fast rise*	1 2/3 tsp.	2 tsp.	3 tsp.
- or -			
Yeast *active dry*	2 1/2 tsp.	3 tsp.	4 tsp.

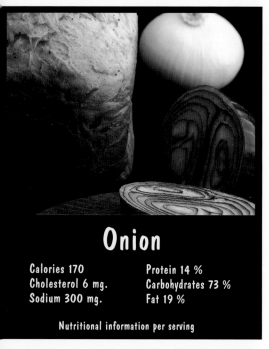

Onion

Calories 170   Protein 14 %
Cholesterol 6 mg.   Carbohydrates 73 %
Sodium 300 mg.   Fat 19 %

Nutritional information per serving

Mary Ann says that when she was baking this bread in the test kitchen, folks would come in off the streets asking, "What *is* this place?" The aroma has that kind of effect, so does the taste. Serve it warm with split pea soup, and your senses will think they've died and gone to heaven.

Success Hints

- Use dried onion flakes, not fresh.

- Old onion bread makes marvelous croutons and bread crumbs. See recipe on page 26.

- This recipe can be baked with the white, rapid, or delay bake cycles.

REGULAR	LARGE	EXTRA LARGE
Water		
3/4 cup	1 1/4 cups	1 1/2 cups
Butter		
1 Tbsp.	2 Tbsp.	2 Tbsp.
White Bread Flour		
2 cups	3 cups	4 cups
Dry Milk		
1 1/2 Tbsp.	2 Tbsp.	3 Tbsp.
Brown Sugar		
1 1/2 Tbsp.	2 Tbsp.	3 Tbsp.
Salt		
1 tsp.	1 1/2 tsp.	2 tsp.
Onions *dried*		
1/4 cup	1/2 cup	1/2 cup
Onion Powder		
1/4 tsp.	1/2 tsp.	1/2 tsp.
Black Pepper		
1/2 tsp.	1 tsp.	1 tsp.
Poppy Seeds		
1/2 tsp.	1 tsp.	1 tsp.
Yeast *fast rise*		
1 tsp.	1 1/2 tsp.	2 tsp.
- or -		
Yeast *active dry*		
2 tsp.	3 tsp.	3 tsp.

Rum Raisin

Calories 181	Protein 13 %
Cholesterol 6 mg.	Carbohydrates 75 %
Sodium 300 mg.	Fat 14 %

Nutritional information per serving

Rum Raisin is another one of those versatile breads that can stretch from breakfast to dessert. Sweeter and richer than our standard raisin bread, Rum Raisin is subtle enough not to be overwhelming while rich enough to stand out. Serve it with our Honey Butter spread for a real treat.

Success Hints

- Soak raisins in spicy or dark rum overnight and drain before using.

- Measure raisins after they have soaked.

- For additional rum flavor add 1/4 teaspoon rum extract. For a non-alcoholic version, pre-soak the raisins in water and use rum extract.

- This recipe can be baked with the white or rapid bake cycles.

REGULAR	LARGE	EXTRA LARGE
Water		
1/2 cup	3/4 cup	7/8 cup
Butter		
2 tsp.	2 Tbsp.	2 Tbsp.
Raisins *pre-soaked in rum*		
1/2 cup	3/4 cup	1 cup
Heavy Cream		
2 Tbsp.	1/4 cup	1/3 cup
White Bread Flour		
2 cups	3 cups	4 cups
Dry Milk		
1 Tbsp.	2 Tbsp.	2 Tbsp.
Brown Sugar		
1 tsp.	2 tsp.	1 Tbsp.
Salt		
1 tsp.	1 1/2 tsp.	2 tsp.
Yeast *fast rise*		
3/4 tsp.	1 1/8 tsp.	1 1/2 tsp.
- or - **Yeast** *active dry*		
1 1/2 tsp.	2 tsp.	2 1/2 tsp.

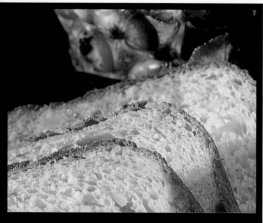

Luscious Luau

Calories 188	**Protein** 10 %	
Cholesterol 1 mg.	**Carbohydrates** 62 %	
Sodium 280 mg.	**Fat** 29 %	

Nutritional information per serving

One bite of this light, sweet loaf and you can feel the tropical breezes. The pineapple and coconut add sweetness and flavor, but the macadamia nuts are the real stars of the show. This is one bread that's better served cool than hot. The pineapple is especially enhanced with cooling. The possibilities for this bread are endless, but we'll tell you this: Luscious Luau makes toast a celestial experience.

Success Hints

■ Drain the pineapple very well.

■ Macadamia nuts add a wonderful texture if added in large chunks. We quarter ours.

■ This is a high rising bread, perfect for the rapid cycle.

■ This recipe can be baked with the white, sweet, or rapid bake cycles.

REGULAR	LARGE	EXTRA LARGE
Water		
1/2 cup	3/4 cup	1 cup
Carrots *shredded*		
2 Tbsp.	3 Tbsp.	1/4 cup
Pineapple *unsweetened crushed*		
1/2 cup	2/3 cup	3/4 cup
White Bread Flour		
2 cups	2 3/4 cups	3 1/2 cups
Dry Milk		
1 tsp.	2 tsp.	1 Tbsp.
Salt		
1 tsp.	1 1/2 tsp.	2 tsp.
Brown Sugar		
1 1/2 Tbsp.	2 Tbsp.	2 Tbsp.
Coconut *flaked/shredded*		
1/4 cup	1/3 cup	1/2 cup
Macadamia Nuts *unsalted, coarsely chopped*		
1/3 cup	1/2 cup	1/2 cup
Cinnamon		
pinch	pinch	1/8 tsp.
Yeast *fast rise*		
1 tsp.	1 1/2 tsp.	1 1/2 tsp.
- or -		
Yeast *active dry*		
2 tsp.	2 tsp.	2 tsp.

Pizza Pleasure

Calories 159
Cholesterol 3 mg.
Sodium 293 mg.

Protein 14 %
Carbohydrates 73 %
Fat 13 %

Nutritional information per serving

In the wintertime, Suzan's son, Martin, likes to have "pizza picnics" on a picnic blanket in front of the fireplace. With this bread, you can take your pizza on a real picnic - it's that close to the real thing. Just toss a loaf in your picnic basket, and you're ready to go. Finally, pizza with a perfect crust!

Success Hints

- Use stick pepperoni and dice into 1/4" chunks.

- As with all cheese breads, loaf appearance will be unusual due to the moisture of the cheese - a small price to pay for great taste.

- This bread can be made with the white or rapid bake cycles.

REGULAR	LARGE	EXTRA LARGE
Water		
3/4 cup	1 1/8 cups	1 1/3 cups
Pepperoni *chopped*		
3 Tbsp.	1/4 cup	1/2 cup
Mozzarella *shredded*		
2 Tbsp.	2 Tbsp.	3 Tbsp.
Mushrooms *canned/drained*		
2 Tbsp.	3 Tbsp.	1/4 cup
White Bread Flour		
2 cups	3 cups	4 cups
Sugar		
1 Tbsp.	2 Tbsp.	2 Tbsp.
Salt		
1 tsp.	1 1/4 tsp.	1 1/2 tsp.
Parmesan *grated*		
2 tsp.	1 Tbsp.	4 tsp.
Onion Flakes		
2 Tbsp.	1/4 cup	1/3 cup
Garlic Powder		
1/2 tsp.	3/4 tsp.	1 tsp.
Oregano		
1/2 tsp.	3/4 tsp.	1 tsp.
Yeast *fast rise*		
1 tsp.	1 1/2 tsp.	1 1/2 tsp.
- or -		
Yeast *active dry*		
2 tsp.	2 tsp.	2 1/2 tsp.

Peaches and Cream

Calories 161
Cholesterol 0 mg.
Sodium 238 mg.

Protein 12 %
Carbohydrates 82 %
Fat 4 %

Nutritional information per serving

You may love your peaches and cream chilled, but the way to serve this lovely light bread is warm from the oven. Like your favorite peach cobbler, the subtle richness of the flavors lends itself perfectly to a light topping of fresh butter. Try it for bread and butter sandwiches and you may decide to make afternoon tea a ritual.

Success Hints

- For a creamy texture, use low fat yogurt; if you're calorie counting, nonfat will do.

- For more of a cobbler effect, increase nutmeg and cinnamon to taste.

- This recipe can be used with the white, sweet or rapid bake cycles.

REGULAR	LARGE	EXTRA LARGE
Water		
1/2 cup	3/4 cup	7/8 cup
Peach Yogurt		
1/3 cup	1/2 cup	2/3 cups
Applesauce		
2 Tbsp.	2 Tbsp.	1/4 cup
White Bread Flour		
1 1/2 cups	2 cups	2 2/3 cups
Whole Wheat Flour		
1/2 cup	1 cup	1 1/3 cups
Dry Milk		
1 Tbsp.	1 1/2 Tbsp.	2 Tbsp.
Brown Sugar		
2 tsp.	1 Tbsp.	1 Tbsp.
Salt		
3/4 tsp.	1 1/4 tsp.	1 1/2 tsp.
Dried Peaches *coarsely diced*		
1/2 cup	3/4 cup	1 cup
Nutmeg		
1/8 tsp.	1/4 tsp.	1/4 tsp.
Cinnamon		
1/8 tsp.	1/4 tsp.	1/2 tsp.
Yeast *fast rise*		
1 1/2 tsp.	1 1/2 tsp.	2 tsp.
- or - **Yeast** *active dry*		
2 tsp.	2 1/2 tsp.	3 tsp.

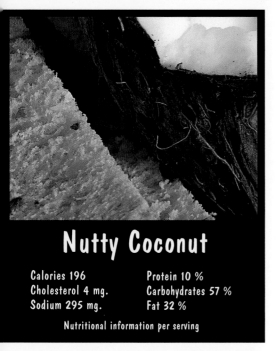

Nutty Coconut

Calories 196
Cholesterol 4 mg.
Sodium 295 mg.

Protein 10 %
Carbohydrates 57 %
Fat 32 %

Nutritional information per serving

This softly subtle bread has a wonderful chewy texture. The coconut, pecans and walnuts make a harmonious trio in morning toast. Or serve this bread freshly baked as an accompaniment to your favorite fruit salad.

Success Hints

- For optimal flavor, use pure canned coconut milk.

- For additional chewy crunch, use shredded coconut.

- This recipe can be made with the white or rapid bake cycles.

REGULAR	LARGE	EXTRA LARGE
Water		
3/4 cup	1 1/8 cups	1 1/3 cups
Butter		
1 Tbsp.	1 1/2 Tbsp.	2 Tbsp.
Cream of Coconut *canned*		
1 Tbsp.	2 Tbsp.	2 Tbsp.
White Bread Flour		
2 cups	3 cups	4 cups
Salt		
1 tsp.	1 1/2 tsp.	2 tsp.
Coconut *flakes or shredded*		
1/4 cup	1/2 cup	1/2 cup
Pecans		
3 Tbsp.	1/4 cup	1/3 cup
Walnuts		
3 Tbsp.	1/4 cup	1/3 cup
Yeast *fast rise*		
1 tsp.	1 1/2 tsp.	1 1/2 tsp.
- or -		
Yeast *active dry*		
2 tsp.	2 tsp.	2 tsp.

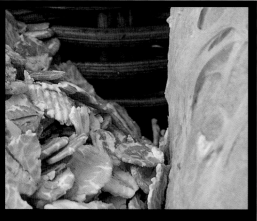

Outrageously Oatmeal

Calories 189 **Protein** 13%
Cholesterol 6 mg. **Carbohydrates** 72 %
Sodium 297 mg. **Fat** 15 %

Nutritional information per serving

There's more than one way to eat your oatmeal. One taste of this full-bodied white bread, and you'll never call it mush again! The light oat taste makes it a natural for hearty morning toast. This nicely textured bread makes fine sandwiches, too.

Success Hints

- For added texture, add the oats after the first knead or at the beep on the fruit and nut cycle.

- For additional crunch, sprinkle a few oats on top of the loaf after the final rise.

- Instant oatmeal doesn't work, but quick-cooking oats do.

- Try with Ginger Pecan Butter - page 143.

- This recipe can be made with the white, rapid, or delay bake cycles.

REGULAR	LARGE	EXTRA LARGE
Water		
3/4 cup	1 cup	1 1/2 cups
Butter		
1 Tbsp.	2 Tbsp.	2 Tbsp.
Honey		
1 Tbsp.	2 Tbsp.	2 Tbsp.
White Bread Flour		
2 cups	3 cups	3 3/4 cups
Dry Milk		
1 Tbsp.	1 1/2 Tbsp.	2 Tbsp.
Salt		
1 tsp.	1 1/2 tsp.	2 tsp.
Rolled Oats		
1/4 cup	1/2 cup	3/4 cup
Yeast *fast rise*		
1 tsp.	2 tsp.	2 tsp.
- or -		
Yeast *active dry*		
1 1/2 tsp.	3 tsp.	3 tsp.

Chocolate Cherry

Calories 163	Protein 12 %
Cholesterol 0 mg.	Carbohydrates 78 %
Sodium 280 mg.	Fat 5 %

Nutritional information per serving

You'll never have to ask the kids to finish their bread again. Paul Swalling, 10 years old, visited the test kitchen and managed to eat a whole loaf before anyone noticed! For adults, Chocolate Cherry turns a coffee break into a pleasant interlude. With a sweet topping, it becomes a new dessert bread.

Success Hints

- Make sure to use real chocolate chips.

- Dried Chukar brand cherries are available in our accessories section. You may use either dried bing or dried tart red cherries in this recipe.

- This is a soft cake-like bread. Cool before slicing.

- This recipe can be made with the white, sweet, rapid, or delay bake cycles.

REGULAR	LARGE	EXTRA LARGE
Water		
3/4 cup	1 1/4 cups	1 1/2 cups
Molasses		
2 Tbsp.	1/4 cup	1/4 cup
Triple Sec		
2 tsp.	1 Tbsp.	4 tsp.
White Bread Flour		
1 1/2 cups	2 cups	3 cups
Whole Wheat Flour		
1/2 cup	1 cup	1 cup
Dry Milk		
1 Tbsp.	2 Tbsp.	2 Tbsp.
Salt		
1 tsp.	1 1/2 tsp.	2 tsp.
Chocolate Chips		
1/3 cup	1/2 cup	2/3 cup
Cherries dried		
1/3 cup	1/2 cup	2/3 cup
Orange Peel		
1/4 tsp.	1/2 tsp.	1/2 tsp.
Yeast fast rise		
1 tsp.	2 tsp.	2 tsp.
- or -		
Yeast active dry		
2 tsp.	3 tsp.	4 tsp.

Fall Harvest

Calories 195　　**Protein 14 %**
Cholesterol 6 mg.　**Carbohydrates 62 %**
Sodium 300 mg.　　**Fat 28 %**

Nutritional information per serving

We originally called this Pumpkin Bread but decided that was too suggestive of pumpkin pie. Rather than sweet, this loaf is a full-bodied squash bread, more reminiscent of acorn squash. The pumpkin seeds are a wonderful, distinctive touch; they give the bread crunch along with a special taste of autumn.

Success Hints

- Be sure to use plain canned pumpkin – not pumpkin pie filling.

- This recipe can be made with the white or rapid bake cycles.

REGULAR	LARGE	EXTRA LARGE
Water		
1/2 cup	1 cup	1 cup
Butter		
1 Tbsp.	2 Tbsp.	2 Tbsp.
Pumpkin *canned*		
1/4 cup	1/2 cup	1/2 cup
Vanilla Extract		
1/2 tsp.	1 tsp.	1 1/2 tsp.
White Bread Flour		
2 cups	3 cups	4 cups
Dry Milk		
1 Tbsp.	2 Tbsp.	2 Tbsp.
Salt		
1 tsp.	1 1/2 tsp.	2 tsp.
Brown Sugar		
1 Tbsp.	2 Tbsp.	2 Tbsp.
Ginger *ground*		
1/2 tsp.	3/4 tsp.	1 tsp.
Nutmeg		
1/2 tsp.	3/4 tsp.	1 tsp.
Pumpkin Seeds		
1/4 cup	1/2 cup	1/2 cup
Yeast *fast rise*		
1 tsp.	1 1/2 tsp.	1 1/2 tsp.
- or -		
Yeast *active dry*		
2 tsp.	2 tsp.	2 tsp.

Tabouli

Calories 102
Cholesterol 35 mg.
Sodium 303 mg.
Protein 12 %
Carbohydrates 73 %
Fat 13 %

Nutritional information per serving

This is a bread that's definitely different. Inspired by the Middle Eastern bulgur wheat dish, this medium bodied loaf offers a unique blending of tastes and textures. Mary, a tabouli lover, says it can't be beat for a meatloaf sandwich. Or try it with a Greek salad or slices of feta cheese.

Success Hints

■ Break egg into liquid measuring cup, then fill with water to the combined egg and water measurement.

■ For additional flavor, add 1/2 tsp. of dried mint leaves.

■ Place apricots away from water.

■ Tabouli mix can be found in the gourmet or health food section.

■ This recipe can be made with the white or rapid bake cycles.

REGULAR	LARGE	EXTRA LARGE
1 Egg plus Water to equal		
3/4 cup	1 1/4 cups	1 1/3 cups
Olive Oil		
1/2 Tbsp.	1 Tbsp.	1 Tbsp.
Yogurt *nonfat*		
2 Tbsp.	1/4 cup	1/4 cup
Black Olives *chopped*		
2 Tbsp.	1/4 cup	1/4 cup
White Bread Flour		
2 cups	3 1/4 cups	4 cups
Sugar		
1 Tbsp.	2 Tbsp.	2 Tbsp.
Salt		
3/4 tsp.	1 1/2 tsp.	1 1/2 tsp.
Apricots *chopped/dried*		
2 Tbsp.	1/4 cup	1/4 cup
Tabouli Mix		
1/4 cup	1/2 cup	1/2 cup
Yeast *fast rise*		
1 tsp.	1 1/2 tsp.	1 1/2 tsp.
- or -		
Yeast *active dry*		
2 tsp.	2 tsp.	3 tsp.

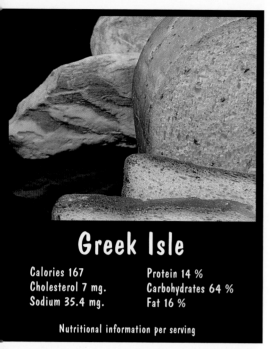

Greek Isle

Calories 167   Protein 14 %
Cholesterol 7 mg.   Carbohydrates 64 %
Sodium 35.4 mg.   Fat 16 %

Nutritional information per serving

Unique is the word for this loaf. Don't let the combination of ingredients scare you off - the texture created by the feta cheese combined with the smallest hint of cucumber makes this a wonderful bread. This is definitely a bread to accompany a hot meal. We recommend it with char-grilled marinated lamb chops or your favorite lamb kabobs.

Success Hints

- Cucumber should be peeled, sliced lengthwise, seeded and then pureed.

- If the feta cheese is packed in water, drain well.

- Finely chop black olives.

- The recipe can be made with the white or rapid bake cycles.

REGULAR	LARGE	EXTRA LARGE
Water		
1/2 cup	3/4 cup	1 cup
Butter		
2 tsp.	1 Tbsp.	4 tsp.
Yogurt *plain*		
3 Tbsp.	1/4 cup	1/3 cup
Black Olives *chopped*		
4 tsp.	2 Tbsp.	3 Tbsp.
Feta Cheese		
2 1/2 Tbsp.	1/4 cup	1/4 cup
Cucumber *pureed*		
2 1/2 Tbsp.	2 Tbsp.	1/4 cup
White Bread Flour		
2 cups	3 cups	4 cups
Dry Milk		
2 tsp.	1 Tbsp.	4 tsp.
Sugar		
1 Tbsp.	1 1/2 Tbsp.	2 Tbsp.
Salt		
1 tsp.	1 1/2 tsp.	2 tsp.
Garlic Powder		
pinch	1/4 tsp.	1/4 tsp.
Sweet Basil		
1/2 tsp.	3/4 tsp.	1 tsp.
Dill Weed		
1/2 tsp.	3/4 tsp.	1 tsp.
Yeast *fast rise*		
1/2 tsp.	3/4 tsp.	1 tsp.
- or -		
Yeast *active dry*		
1 tsp.	1 1/2 tsp.	2 tsp.

Sun Nut

Calories 207
Cholesterol 6 mg.
Sodium 299 mg.

Protein 14 %
Carbohydrates 64 %
Fat 25 %

Nutritional information per serving

This is a bread to make sunflower lovers sing. The sunflower seeds impart a lovely, subtle taste and a lovely chewy texture. Toasted, this bread does wonderful things with fruit and jelly, and it will breathe new life into that predictable cheese sandwich.

Success Hints

- This bread makes croutons with a new kind of crunch. See our recipe on page 26.

- Sunflower seed salt content varies by brand. If using low or unsalted seeds, adjust salt accordingly.

- This recipe can be made with the white, rapid, or delay bake cycles.

	REGULAR	LARGE	EXTRA LARGE
Water	3/4 cup	1 1/4 cups	1 1/2 cups
Butter	1 Tbsp.	2 Tbsp.	2 Tbsp.
Honey	2 Tbsp.	3 Tbsp.	1/4 cup
White Bread Flour	1 3/4 cups	2 1/2 cups	3 1/2 cups
Whole Wheat Flour	1/2 cup	3/4 cup	1 cup
Dry Milk	1 Tbsp.	2 Tbsp.	2 Tbsp.
Salt	1 tsp.	1 1/2 tsp.	2 tsp.
Sunflower Seeds	1/4 cup	1/2 cup	1/2 cup
Yeast *fast rise*	1 1/4 tsp.	1 1/4 tsp.	1 1/4 tsp.
- or -			
Yeast *active dry*	2 tsp.	2 1/2 tsp.	3 tsp.

Bleu Cheese & Port

Calories 181   Protein 13 %
Cholesterol 5 mg.   Carbohydrates 62 %
Sodium 334 mg.   Fat 23 %

Nutritional information per serving

Whether bleu or blue, there are no two ways about it - a blue cheese lover will love this bread. This moderately textured loaf makes great croutons and wonderful toast points for parties. Or serve it warm with your favorite steak.

Success Hints

- No need to use an expensive port here, just one with good flavor.

- The sharper the blue cheese, the stronger the flavor in the bread. We like the Danish blue best.

- As with all cheese recipes, loaf appearance may vary but the flavor is worth it.

- This recipe can be made with the white or rapid bake cycles.

REGULAR	LARGE	EXTRA LARGE
Water		
2/3 cup	1 cup	1 1/4 cups
Butter		
2 tsp.	1 Tbsp.	1 Tbsp.
Port Red Wine		
2 Tbsp.	1/4 cup	1/4 cup
Blue Cheese		
1/4 cup	1/3 cup	1/3 cup
Applesauce		
1 Tbsp.	2 Tbsp.	2 Tbsp.
White Bread Flour		
2 cups	3 cups	4 cups
Sugar		
1 Tbsp.	2 Tbsp.	2 Tbsp.
Salt		
1 tsp.	1 1/2 tsp.	2 tsp.
Walnuts *coarsely chopped*		
1/4 cup	1/3 cup	1/2 cup
Yeast *fast rise*		
3/4 tsp.	1 tsp.	1 1/2 tsp.
- or - **Yeast** *active dry*		
1 1/2 tsp.	1 1/2 tsp.	2 tsp.

Sourdough White

Calories 169   **Protein** 13 %
Cholesterol 6 mg.   **Carbohydrates** 71 %
Sodium 290 mg.   **Fat** 14 %

Nutritional information per serving

REGULAR	LARGE	EXTRA LARGE
Starter		
1 1/2 cups	2 cups	3 cups
Butter		
1 Tbsp.	2 Tbsp.	2 Tbsp.
White Bread Flour		
1 1/2 cups	2 cups	3 cups
Dry Milk		
1 Tbsp.	2 Tbsp.	2 Tbsp.
Sugar		
1 Tbsp.	2 Tbsp.	2 Tbsp.
Salt		
1 tsp.	1 1/2 tsp.	2 tsp.
Yeast *fast rise*		
1 tsp.	2 tsp.	2 tsp.
- *or* -		
Yeast *active dry*		
2 tsp.	3 tsp.	4 tsp.

If you're in the pioneering spirit, here's a Sourdough for you. Yes, sourdough *is* possible in a bread machine - for bakers with the time, patience and adventuresome spirit to see this most independent bread to completion. Because every starter is different, sourdough baking is always a challenge. In bread machines, it becomes its own art form. Experiment - it's the hallmark of a Sourdough baker!

Success Hints

- Follow preparation instructions for your chosen starter. Starter may take 24 hours to 4 days to activate.

- To ensure proper balance, always feed your starter equal parts flour and water (85°).

- We baked our Sourdough successes on the white cycle.

- Timing and temperature are the key elements of success.
  * Careful observation will reveal your starter's peaking schedule. Starter should be peaking when loaded into machine, frothy and bubbly, not just foamy.
  * Optimum room temperature for culture activation and machine baking is 85°.

- If starter peaks at an inconvenient time, store it in the refrigerator. Re-activate by feeding again and placing in an 85-95° place for 6-12 hours.

- Save some of the active starter for your next batch. Refrigerate in an airtight container.

- Sourdough starters are available in our accessories section.

Banana Granola

Calories 192   Protein 12 %
Cholesterol 6 mg.   Carbohydrates 65 %
Sodium 297 mg.   Fat 26 %

Nutritional information per serving

This is a fairly heavy, moist bread that's not as sweet as the ingredients might suggest. The fruit and granola combine to make a slightly nutty taste with a hint of banana. This bread makes terrific toast with a hearty breakfast of bacon and eggs.

Success Hints

- This dough will be sticky, resist the urge to add flour.

- This bread is wonderful with the Honey Butter - page 143.

- Use your favorite granola mix for your own personalized flavor.

- This recipe can be made with the white, whole wheat or rapid bake cycles.

	REGULAR	LARGE	EXTRA LARGE
Water	2/3 cup	1 cup	1 1/4 cups
Butter	4 tsp.	2 Tbsp.	3 Tbsp.
Bananas *sliced*	1/2 cup	1/2 cup	1 cup
Molasses	1 Tbsp.	2 Tbsp.	3 Tbsp.
White Bread Flour	1 1/4 cups	2 cups	2 2/3 cups
Whole Wheat Flour	3/4 cup	1 cup	1 1/3 cups
Dry Milk	1 1/2 tsp.	1 Tbsp.	2 Tbsp.
Salt	1 tsp.	1 1/2 tsp.	2 tsp.
Granola	1/2 cup	3/4 cup	1 cup
Walnuts *chopped*	1/4 cup	1/3 cup	1/2 cup
Bananas Chips *dried*	1/4 cup	1/3 cup	1/2 cup
Yeast *fast rise*	1 tsp.	1 1/2 tsp.	2 tsp.
- or -			
Yeast *active dry*	1 tsp.	1 1/2 tsp.	2 tsp.

Tangy Cranberry

Calories 189   Protein 11 %
Cholesterol 5 mg.   Carbohydrates 76 %
Sodium 301 mg.   Fat 13 %

Nutritional information per serving

Wanna bet there's nothing new to do with that leftover turkey? This moist, light bread promises to redefine your idea of a turkey sandwich. But don't stop there. Try a slice of sharp cheddar with a little English mustard. Experiment - and enjoy.

REGULAR	LARGE	EXTRA LARGE
Cranberry Juice		
3/4 cup	1 1/4 cups	1 1/2 cups
Butter		
1 Tbsp.	2 Tbsp.	2 Tbsp.
Orange Marmalade		
2 Tbsp.	3 Tbsp.	1/4 cup
White Bread Flour		
2 cups	3 cups	4 cups
Dry Milk		
1 Tbsp.	2 Tbsp.	2 Tbsp.
Salt		
1 tsp.	1 1/2 tsp.	2 tsp.
Cranberries *dried*		
1/4 cup	1/3 cup	1/2 cup
Yeast *fast rise*		
1 tsp.	2 tsp.	2 tsp.
- or -		
Yeast *active dry*		
2 tsp.	3 tsp.	4 tsp.

Success Hints

■ Chukar brand dried cranberries are available in our accessories section. Gourmet stores and specialty food catalogs also carry dried cranberries.

■ Place dried cranberries away from water if using the delay bake cycle.

■ This recipe can be baked with the white or delay bake cycles.

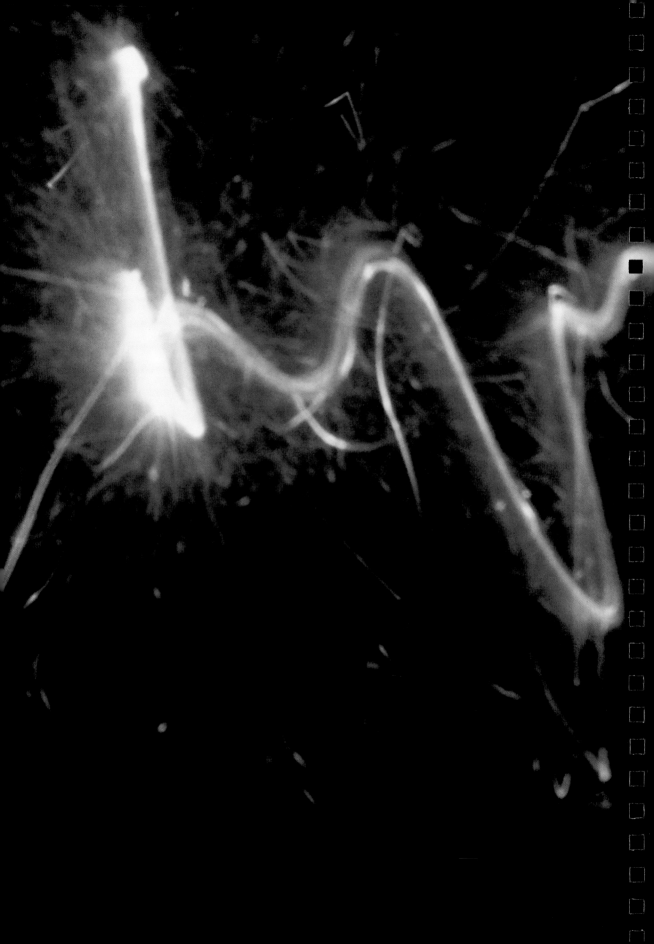

SPECIALTY BREADS

These festive recipes combine the
ease of machine preparation with
the satisfying creativity of baking.
Your machine mixes and kneads
the dough, then you form it and
bake it in your regular oven.
Surprise your friends with new
shapes of electric bread!

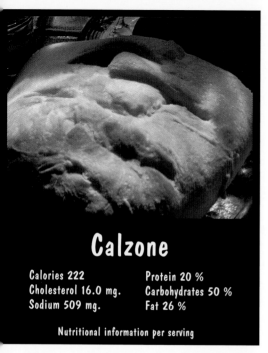

Calzone

Calories 222
Cholesterol 16.0 mg.
Sodium 509 mg.

Protein 20 %
Carbohydrates 50 %
Fat 26 %

Nutritional information per serving

		SIZE A One Calzone 8 slices	SIZE B Two Calzone 16 slices
3/4 cup	Water		1 1/2 cups
2 cups	White Bread Flour		4 cups
1/2 tsp.	Dry Milk		1 tsp.
1 Tbsp.	Sugar		2 Tbsp.
1/2 tsp.	Salt		1 tsp.
1 tsp.	Yeast *fast rise*		2 tsp.
	- or -		
2 tsp.	Yeast *active dry*		4 tsp.

Think of Calzone as an elegant alternative to pizza. Your choice of fillings is limited only by your imagination; dress it up for a buffet or make it a simple one course family meal.

Success Hints

■ Calzone can be prepared several hours ahead of time and kept in the refrigerator until baking time.

■ Double the pizza sauce recipe and drizzle warm sauce over the Calzone before serving.

■ Add pesto to pizza sauce if you like extra garlic and basil.

Remove dough from the machine after the dough or manual cycle is completed, then follow the process steps below.

	FILLING	
1/2 cup	Pizza Sauce	3/4 cup
1/2 cup	Italian Sausage *cooked/crumbled*	3/4 cup
1 cup	Mozzarella Cheese *shredded*	1 1/4 cups
	Chop the following and add	
1/4 cup	Feta Cheese	1/3 cup
3 oz.	Pepperoni	6 oz.
1/4 cup	Green Peppers	1/2 cup
1/4 cup	Onions	1/2 cup
1/8 cup	Olives	1/4 cup

Remove dough to a lightly floured surface. For Size B, cut into two equal portions and prepare each calzone as follows: Roll dough to a 16 x 10 rectangle. Transfer to lightly greased cookie sheet. Spoon pizza sauce onto center of dough, and add filling. Make diagonal cuts 1 1/2 inches apart down each side, cutting to within a half inch of the filling. Crisscross strips of dough over filling, pressing down and sealing with a drop of water. Brush top with melted butter and bake at 350° 35-45 minutes until golden brown.

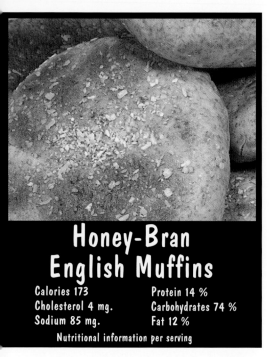

Honey-Bran English Muffins

Calories 173
Cholesterol 4 mg.
Sodium 85 mg.

Protein 14 %
Carbohydrates 74 %
Fat 12 %

Nutritional information per serving

SIZE A 8 Muffins		SIZE B 12 Muffins
3/4 cup	**Water**	1 1/4 cups
1 Tbsp.	**Butter**	2 Tbsp.
2 Tbsp.	**Honey**	3 Tbsp.
2 cups	**White Bread Flour**	3 cups
1/4 tsp.	**Salt**	1/2 tsp.
1/2 cup	**Wheat Bran** *cereal bits*	3/4 cup
1 Tbsp.	**Oat Bran**	1 1/2 Tbsp.
1 tsp.	**Yeast** *fast rise*	2 tsp.
	- or -	
2 tsp.	**Yeast** *active dry*	3 tsp.

Slightly sweet and nutty, these English muffins stick to your ribs without being too heavy. Try them toasted with our Guava-Raisin spread on page 143.

Remove dough from the machine after the dough or manual cycle is completed, then follow the process steps below.

Success Hints

- For Raisin Muffins, add 1/4 cup of raisins and 1/2 tsp. of cinnamon for Size A, or prepare Size B using 1/3 cup of raisins and 2/3 tsp. of cinnamon.

Turn dough out onto floured surface. Divide into 8 portions for Size A and 12 for Size B. Shape each into a ball, then press into 4" circles about 3/4" high. Grease baking sheet and sprinkle with half the oat bran, then place muffins 2" apart. Spritz with water and sprinkle with remaining bran. Let rise until doubled, about an hour. Grease electric skillet or griddle and preheat to 325° or medium heat. Carefully place muffins in skillet, then cook about 6 minutes on each side or until brown. Cool.

Saffron Braids

Calories 186
Cholesterol 22 mg.
Sodium 325 mg.

Protein 13 %
Carbohydrates 67 %
Fat 19 %

Nutritional information per serving

	SIZE A 1 Large Braid Serves 10		SIZE B 2 Braids Serves 16
1 1/4 cups	Water	1 1/2 cups
1	Egg	1
2 Tbsp.	Olive Oil	3 Tbsp.
3 cups	White Bread Flour	4 cups
1/2 Tbsp.	Sugar	2 tsp.
1 1/2 tsp.	Salt	2 tsp.
1/2 tsp.	Saffron ground	1/2 tsp.
	-or-	
1/4 tsp.	Saffron threads	1/4 tsp.
2 tsp.	Yeast fast rise	2 tsp.
	- or -	
3 tsp.	Yeast active dry	4 tsp.

As beautiful as it is exotic, this bread is a genuinely unique addition to any dinner party. Because the dough is prepared in the machine, this succulent centerpiece takes surprisingly little time to prepare.

Remove dough from the machine after the dough or manual cycle is completed, then follow the process steps below.

Success Hints

■ If using saffron threads, grind with mortar and pestle. It does not need to be a fine powder.

Turn dough out onto floured surface (it will be sticky) and punch down. For Size B, cut dough in half to make two braids. Prepare each braid as follows: Divide and make three ropes about 9 - 12 " long. Pinch ropes together at one end, braid, and pinch together at other end to secure braid. Transfer to greased baking sheet, let rise until double in size, about one hour. Brush with beaten egg and sprinkle with sesame seeds. Bake at 375° for 20-25 minutes.

Fruit Spiral

Calories 302   Protein 8 %
Cholesterol 33 mg.   Carbohydrates 80 %
Sodium 225 mg.   Fat 11 %

Nutritional information per serving

This festive brunch offering takes a little time - but not nearly as much as your guests will think! Filled with peach, apple, cherry or berry filling it becomes the center of attention.

Success Hints

- Use the whole fruit and pieces with just a little sauce from the filling.

- Drizzle top with white icing for special effects.

SIZE A One Spiral Serves 8		SIZE B Two Spirals Serves 16
3/4 cup	**Water**	1 1/2 cups
1 1/2 Tbsp.	**Butter**	3 Tbsp.
1	**Egg**	1
2 cups	**White Bread Flour**	4 cups
1 Tbsp.	**Dry Milk**	2 Tbsp.
1 1/2 Tbsp.	**Sugar**	3 Tbsp.
1/2 tsp.	**Salt**	1 tsp.
3/4 tsp.	**Coriander** *ground*	1 tsp.
1 1/2 tsp.	**Lemon Peel** *dried*	2 tsp.
1 tsp.	**Yeast** *fast rise*	2 tsp.
	- or -	
2 tsp.	**Yeast** *active dry*	4 tsp.

	FILLING	
1/2 Can	**Prepared Pie Filling**	1 Can

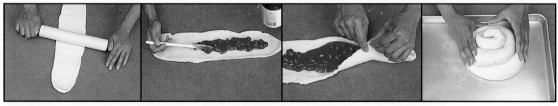

Turn dough out onto lightly floured surface and punch down. For Size B, divide dough into two equal portions. Prepare each spiral as follows: Chill in refrigerator sealed in an airtight plastic bag for 2 hours or overnight. Roll on floured surface and stretch dough into thin strip, 5 - 6" wide and 30" long. (Keep board floured.) Place fruit and sauce down the middle. Brush edge with water, fold over into a tube, sealing filling inside. Coiling from one end, form 5 - 7" circle with seam inside. Coil remaining dough, gradually spiraling narrower and higher. Transfer to greased baking sheet and let rise until double, about one hour. Brush with beaten egg. Bake at 325° for 30 minutes. Then cover with foil to prevent over-browning, and continue baking for 30 minutes more.

Orange Kisses

Calories 328	Protein 10 %
Cholesterol 41 mg.	Carbohydrates 51 %
Sodium 304 mg.	Fat 44 %

Nutritional information per serving

Ann's mother, Wanda Thompson, used to make these festive fruit rolls for holidays. For years, Ann "cheated" with time-saving frozen bread dough to imitate her mother's recipe. Now Ann uses her bread machine to pass the tradition along to her daughters. The sugar bakes with the orange rind and butter to create a crispy, crunchy top – and a decadently gooey bottom.

Success Hints

- Use only the orange portion of the orange rind.

SIZE A 8 Rolls		SIZE B 16 Rolls
3/4 cup	**Water**	1 1/2 cups
2 Tbsp.	**Butter**	4 Tbsp.
2 cups	**White Bread Flour**	4 cups
1/2 Tbsp.	**Orange Peel** *dried*	1 Tbsp.
1 1/2 Tbsp.	**Dry Milk**	3 Tbsp.
2 Tbsp.	**Sugar**	4 Tbsp.
1/2 tsp.	**Salt**	1 tsp.
1 tsp.	**Yeast** *fast rise*	2 tsp.
	- or -	
2 tsp.	**Yeast** *active dry*	4 tsp.

Remove dough from the machine after the dough or manual cycle is completed. Then remove and follow the process steps below.

COATING		
1/2 cup	**Butter** *softened*	3/4 cup
1 1/2 Tbsp.	**Orange Rind** *fresh grated*	3 Tbsp.
1/2 cup	**Sugar**	1 cup

Turn dough out onto a lightly floured surface and form a large ball. Divide Size A into 8 portions, and 16 for Size B. Form into balls, and coat each ball with softened butter. Roll in orange-sugar mixture. Place 8 balls into a 9" pie pan. Let rise until dough doubles, about one hour. Bake at 350° 25-30 minutes until just golden brown.

Sticky Buns

Calories 304
Cholesterol 37 mg.
Sodium 271 mg.

Protein 10 %
Carbohydrates 46 %
Fat 49 %

Nutritional information per serving

SIZE A 9 Buns		SIZE B 15 Buns
3/4 cup	**Water**	1 1/4 cups
2 Tbsp.	**Butter**	3 Tbsp.
2 cups	**White Bread Flour**	3 cups
1 1/2 Tbsp.	**Dry Milk**	2 Tbsp.
2 Tbsp.	**Sugar**	3 Tbsp.
1/2 tsp.	**Salt**	1 tsp.
1 tsp.	**Yeast** *fast rise*	2 tsp.
	- or -	
2 tsp.	**Yeast** *active dry*	3 tsp.

Is there anything like homemade sticky buns? Kids love to help roll out the dough and add the nuts. Let it become one of *their* specialities!

Remove dough from the machine after the dough or manual cycle is completed, then follow the process steps below.

STICKY SAUCE		
1/4 cup	**Butter**	1/3 cup
1/2 cup	**Brown Sugar**	3/4 cup
1/4 cup	**Corn Syrup** *light*	1/4 cup
1/4 cup	**Pecans** *broken*	1/4 cup

Warm over medium heat until sugar dissolves.

FILLING		
1/4 cup	**Soft Butter**	1/3 cup
1/2 tsp.	**Cinnamon**	1 tsp.

Prepare sticky sauce and pour into 8 x 8 pan for Size A and a 13 x 9 pan for Size B. Sprinkle with broken nuts. Turn dough out onto floured surface (it will be sticky), and punch down. Roll dough to a 16 x 10 rectangle for Size B and a 12 x 8 for Size A. Dot with soft butter and sprinkle with cinnamon. Roll jellyroll style and pinch seams together. Slice into 1 1/2" thick pieces, place into pan on top of sticky sauce, and let double in size, about one hour. Bake at 350° for 25-30 minutes. Cool for no more than three minutes, then invert pan so sauce and nuts are on top of buns.

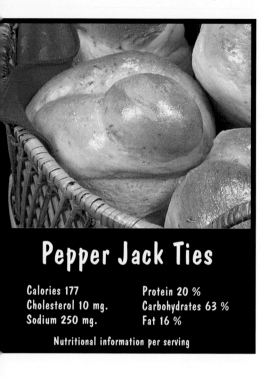

Pepper Jack Ties

Calories 177
Cholesterol 10 mg.
Sodium 250 mg.
Protein 20 %
Carbohydrates 63 %
Fat 16 %

Nutritional information per serving

These are dinner rolls with a difference - a little kick and a whole lot of flavor. They're best served warm.

Success Hints

- Try replacing cilantro with another favorite herb...dill, rosemary or even crushed black pepper.

SIZE A 8 Rolls		SIZE B 12 Rolls
3/4 cup	**Water**	1 1/4 cups
1/2 cup	**Pepper Jack Cheese**	3/4 cup
2 cups	**White Bread Flour**	3 cups
1 1/2 tsp.	**Dry Milk**	1/2 Tbsp.
1 Tbsp.	**Sugar**	2 Tbsp.
1/2 tsp.	**Salt**	1 tsp.
1/2 tsp.	**Red Peppers** *dried/crushed*	1 tsp.
2 tsp.	**Cilantro** *dried*	3 tsp.
1 tsp.	**Yeast** *fast rise*	2 tsp.
	- or -	
2 tsp.	**Yeast** *active dry*	3 tsp.

Remove dough from the machine after the dough or manual cycle is completed, then follow the process steps below.

Turn dough onto lightly floured surface. Punch down and divide dough into 12 parts for Size B, and 8 parts for Size A. Roll each piece into a 7" rope and tie in knot. Place in greased muffin tin or on a cookie sheet and allow to rise for 25 minutes. Brush with egg, and bake at 350° for 20 - 25 minutes.

Picnic Basket

Calories 173
Cholesterol 0 mg.
Sodium 325 mg.

Protein 14 %
Carbohydrates 81 %
Fat 4 %

Nutritional information for 2 oz. serving without chicken

		SIZE A Holds 6 pieces of chicken	SIZE B Holds 8 pieces of chicken
1 1/2 cups	**Water**	1 1/2 cups
3 1/4 cups	**White Bread Flour**	4 cups
1 1/2 Tbsp.	**Sugar**	2 Tbsp.
1 1/2 tsp.	**Salt**	2 tsp.
2 tsp.	**Yeast** *fast rise*	2 tsp.
- or -		
3 tsp.	**Yeast** *active dry*	3 tsp.

Lynn's mother, Virginia Alexander, invented this ingenious dish years ago after her teenagers lost too many kitchen containers at the beach. With this oh-so-easy recipe, you bake your own basket - and then eat it!

Success Hints

■ Use to make edible soup bowls. Size A yields three bowls and Size B makes four.

Remove dough from the machine after the dough or manual cycle is completed, then follow the process steps below.

Turn dough out onto lightly floured surface, and carefully form into a ball without punching down. Place onto greased cookie sheet and let rise about one hour until double in size. Brush with beaten egg and bake at 350° for 30 - 35 minutes until golden brown. Let cool. Hollow out cooled bread like a pumpkin, reserving "lid" to put back on. Butter inside and fill with fried chicken. Replace lid and wrap in heavy duty foil, then newspaper, then foil again. Bread and chicken will stay warm all day. All you need is a sunny day, a few ants and some sand!

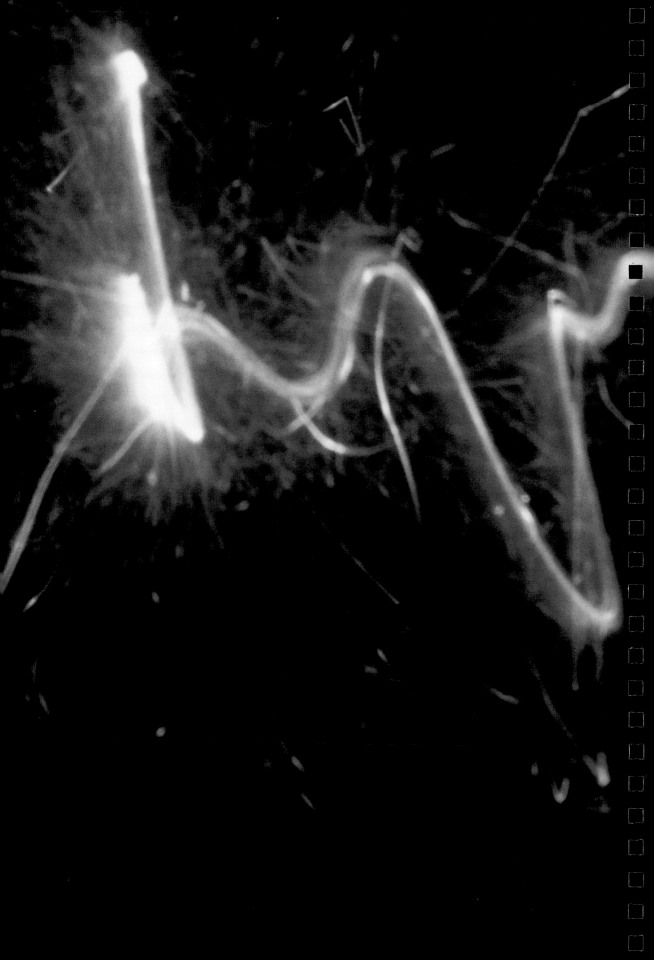

UNIQUE SPREADS, TROUBLESHOOTING & ACCESSORIES

Here's a trio of topics to help you get the most from your machine. Our sweet and savory spreads can enhance any bread - and they're so easy! The Troubleshooting section aims to help you avoid the most common mistakes. And our assortment of handy accessories will make bread baking easier and more fun than ever.

SPREADS
Some are Savory......

Zippy Blue Cheese

3/4 C.   Crumbled Blue Cheese
1 C.   Creamed Cottage Cheese
1/2 C.   Butter or Margarine
1 tsp.   Fresh Basil
1 1/2 tsp.   Oregano Leaves
1 tsp.   Chili Powder
1/4 tsp.   Ground White Pepper

Blend together and store in refrigerator.

Lemon Mustard Butter

1/2 C.   Sweet Butter or Margarine
2 T.   Lemon Juice
1/2 tsp.   Grated Fresh Lemon Rind
1 1/2 T.   Dijon Mustard
Salt and Pepper to taste

Blend together and store in refrigerator.

Jezebel Jam

1/4 C.   Prepared Horseradish
12-oz Jar   Peach-Pineapple Jam
12-oz Jar   Apple Jelly
2 T.   Dry Mustard
1 T.   Ground White Pepper

Mix well and store in refrigerator.

Tarragon-Salmon Spread

1/2 C.   Canned Salmon
1/4 C.   Smoked Salmon
1/2 C.   Butter or Margarine
2 tsp.   Dried Tarragon
1/8 C.   Vodka
Salt and Pepper to taste

Blend together and store in refrigerator.

Chive Roquefort

1/4 C.   Cream Cheese
1/2 C.   Crumbled Roquefort
1/2 C.   Butter or Margarine
2 1/2 T.   Chopped Fresh Chives
1 T.   Lemon Juice
Salt and Pepper to taste

Blend together and store in refrigerator.

Curried Butter

1/2 C.   Butter or Margarine
3/4 tsp.   Curry Powder
1/8 tsp.   Paprika
Dash   Fresh Ground Pepper

Blend together and store in refrigerator.

Hot Chili & Garlic Butter

1/2 C.   Butter or Margarine
1 T.   Prepared Garlic
1 1/4 T.   Red Pepper Flakes
Salt to taste

Blend together and store in refrigerator.

Caraway Blue Cheese

1/3 C.   Crumbled Blue Cheese
3 oz.   Cream Cheese
1/3 C.   Mayonnaise
1 1/2 tsp.   Caraway Seed
White Pepper to taste

Blend together and store in refrigerator.

Green Peppercorn Butter

3 T.   Minced Shallots
3 T.   Butter
3 T.   Brandy
2 T.   Chopped Green Peppercorns
2 tsp.   Dijon Mustard
1/2 C.   Soft Butter or Margarine
1/4 C.   Sour Cream
1   Bouillon Cube (crushed)

Saute shallots in 3 T. butter until gold in color.
Add brandy and reduce by half on high heat.
Add bouillon, peppercorns, and mustard.
When cool mix with butter and cream. Store
in refrigerator.

Some are Sweet........

Ginger-Pecan Butter

3/4 C. Sweet Butter or Margarine
1/2 C. Pecans, finely ground
2 T. Ground Crystallized Ginger
1 tsp. Brown Sugar
1/2 tsp. Allspice

Mix together and store in refrigerator.

Orange-Honey Butter

1 C. Butter, softened
1/3 C. Honey
1 T. Grated Fresh Orange Peel
1 T. Orange Juice Frozen Concentrate

Blend together and store in refrigerator.

Guava-Raisin Spread

1 C. Raisins
2/3 C. Water
1 tsp. Dry Mustard
1 1/2 T. Grated Fresh Orange Peel
1 C. Guava Jelly

Boil raisins and water until water is absorbed, mixing well. Stir in other ingredients. Re-heat, mixing well. Cool then store in refrigerator.

Honey Butter

3/4 C. Butter or Margarine
3/4 C. Honey
3/4 C. Powdered Sugar
1 tsp. Cinnamon

Mix or blend together and store in refrigerator.

Brie Walnut Spread

3/4 C. Brie
1/2 C. Cream Cheese
2 T. Kirsch Liqueur
1/2 C. Walnut Pieces

Blend cheeses and Kirsch together in food processor. Stir in nuts. Store in refrigerator.

Simple Chutney Cheese

1 8-oz. pkg. Cream Cheese
1 C. Apple Chutney
Store bought

Mix together and store in refrigerator.

Cheesy Lemon

2 Eggs, slightly beaten
1/4 C. Lemon Juice
3 T. Butter or Margarine
3/4 C. Sugar
1 tsp. Grated Fresh Lemon Peel
Dash Salt
1 3-oz. pkg. Cream Cheese

In heavy pan mix eggs, juice, butter, sugar and salt. Bring to a boil while stirring over low heat, then cook 3 minutes more. Beat cream cheese and lemon peel. When egg mixture is cool, blend into cheese until smooth and store in refrigerator.

Paskha

2 Egg Yolks
1/2 C. Raisins
1/4 C. Rum
1/4 C. Butter
1 C. Powdered Sugar
1 tsp. Vanilla
zest of 1 Lemon
1 6-oz. pkg Cream Cheese
1/2 C. Toasted Almonds slivered

Soak raisins in rum overnight. Blend butter and cream cheese, add egg yolks, powdered sugar, lemon and vanilla. Fold in raisins, rum and almonds. Chill overnight.

Gruyere Apple Spread

1 6-oz. pkg. Cream Cheese
1 C. Shredded Gruyere Cheese
1 T. Milk
1 1/2 tsp. Prepared Mustard
1/2 C. Shredded, Peeled Apple
1 1/2 tsp. Chopped Chives

Beat cream cheese, blend in gruyere, milk and mustard. Stir in remaining ingredients.

TROUBLESHOOTING

Okay, we admit it: In baking 25,000 test loaves, we experienced a few failures. We've had our share of whole wheat door stops and pumpernickel hockey pucks. We've had loaves that caved in like the Grand Canyon, and loaves that expanded into mushrooms so airy we were tempted to tether them over the test kitchen like helium balloons.

But you know what? Most of those duds were not caused by machine malfunction, they were caused by human error.

Almost always, it came down to ingredients. Although bread machines are forgiving, they also are dependent on a consistent balance of ingredients. The more you use your home bakery, the more you'll develop an instinct for the balance your particular machine requires with your chosen recipes, flours and yeasts. Remember, flour can vary from year to year as the weather and wheat crops change. Yeast is a living organism and occasionally a bottle may have more or less strength than usual.

With some mistakes, there's not much to do but start over. If you put in two tablespoons of salt instead of sugar, or left out the yeast, just be happy you spent minutes instead of hours on this loaf of bread. We'd like to share some tips we picked up along the way, so you can avoid some of our mistakes - and get right to the fun of making your own.

What works or doesn't will vary from one loaf to the next - flours, liquid adjustments, even babysitting. It may help to make notes on a "sticky pad," if you don't want to write in your book, and keep them right on the page of the recipe you're fine-tuning.

On the following pages, we talk about gnarly loaves, pudding pockets, mushroom bread, and even dirty dancing.

Relax. This is easier than it sounds.

Right: These loaves were products of too much going on in our test kitchen at one time. Keeping a close eye on measurements will keep mistakes like these to a minimum.

BREAD WITH CHARACTER - *Looks Can Be Deceiving*

Most often, these loaves "with character" still taste great. Don't be alarmed at producing a loaf that's not perfect every time. Unless Martha Stewart is showing up for your dinner party in 20 minutes, don't stew over it.

Examples of great bread with character.

The five loaves pictured here all have extra "character" - and they all had wonderful flavor and texture. Some even had extra crunchy crust. With the exception of the cratered cheese bread (where reducing the liquid should help), just enjoy it and continue your quest for the "perfect loaf" next time.

PUDDING POCKETS - *The soft-hearted bread*

The Problem: The center of this loaf isn't cooked all the way through.
What To Do:
- Typically it happens with heavier flours such as whole wheat, rye and bran. One solution is an extra knead. After the first knead, let the dough rise, then restart the machine at the very beginning as for a new loaf of bread. That puts more air into the dough.
- Another culprit may be moist ingredients such as yogurt, applesauce, canned chilies and canned fruit. Try reducing your liquids a tablespoon at a time.
- Some rapid cycles which produce bread in two hours or less simply are too short to completely bake a rich gourmet recipe with lots of ingredients.

CRATERED BREAD - *From wet and wild ingredients*

Controlled test bake using too much water.

The Problem: If the top or sides cave in, you've probably got substantially too much moisture.
What To Do:
- Try reducing your water by 1/8 cup.
- Drain canned fruit or vegetables well, and blot dry.
- Promptly remove bread after baking.
- Did you leave out a cup of flour?
- With cheese breads, getting the liquid content right can be tricky, since each cheese has its own moisture content.

ROCKY MOUNTAIN HIGH - *Altitude can give your bread an attitude.*

The Problem: Live in a higher altitude? Your loaves may rise, look great - and then crash while baking. The low air pressure in higher altitudes means your yeast meets with less resistance, so your bread may make promises it can't keep - the bread can't sustain its own expansion.

What To Do:
- Experiment with reducing your yeast 1/4 teaspoon at a time.
- Try reducing water by no more than 1/8 cup.
- Our Colorado-based baker also solved this problem by using a light, finely milled flour, which produced perfect loaves.

MUSHROOM BREAD - *Keeping your yeast under control.*

The Problem: There's too much yeast, it's blown its top, it's officially overproofed.

What To Do:
- Are you using the right yeast with the right measurement? Our recipes give you two yeast measurements. Use either active dry or fast rise - not both!
- Did you use a tablespoon by accident? Yeast is almost always measured in teaspoons.
- You may have too much sugar, or ingredients with natural sugar like dried fruit. Older dried fruit has a higher sugar content. Decrease the sugar accordingly.

Controlled test bake using too much yeast and sugar.

- Another possibility is a smidge too much water. Try decreasing it by one table-spoon at a time. Occasionally, finely ground, softer flours require slightly less water or yeast than the harder, heavier flours.
- If you've checked all of the above, and a recipe still consistently explodes in your machine, try this: replace 1/4 of the total flour with whole wheat flour or add 1/4 teaspoon of fresh lemon juice to the recipe.

GNARLY LOAVES - *Can I buy you a drink?*

The Problem: You know the kind...they look like gnarly tree bark.

What To Do:
- Your dough probably needs more moisture; when it's too dry it can't knead properly. Try reducing the flour 1/8 cup at a time or increasing liquids 1 tablespoon at a time until you hit the right balance for your machine, flour and yeast.

HOME ALONE - *The benefits of babysitting your loaf*

A little babysitting, and your loaf is less likely to get into trouble than if you leave it home alone. Sure, all you really *have* to do is dump in the ingredients and push the button. But, with a little more effort, you can help assure consistently great results. We're not talking here about planting and milling the wheat. Just a little attention on each end of the machine's processing is worth the effort.

Play Ball!

- Learn to "judge" your dough. Unless otherwise noted, most recipes form a ball of dough around the mixing blade, that is smooth, satiny, and feels slightly sticky when touched.

- Is the dough ball too wet or too dry? In addition to possible mis-measurement, variations in humidity, temperature and ingredients can result in an incorrect liquid/flour ratio. Checking the dough ball in the first few minutes can save

Left alone during kneading, this loaf's flavor ended up outside of the loaf!

the loaf, and maybe dinner - add a little extra water (by the teaspoon) if it's too dry, a little extra flour (by the tablespoon) if it's too sticky.

- Are your ingredients mixed in? Check to make sure all the ingredients have been pulled into the dough by the kneading blade. If they're not, use a rubber spatula to carefully push the ingredients into the dough.

- On very hot, humid days, you may also want to reduce the water by two tablespoons, watch the dough, then add water one teaspoon at a time, as needed, until it is a silky smooth ball.

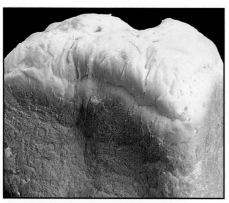

Left unattended, this loaf collapsed in the pan after it was done baking.

Hot to Trot!
Take your bread out of the machine promptly when it's done baking.

- A hot loaf left to steam in a warm pan can result in soggy sides and silly shapes.

- Bread crusts, particularly sweet ones with their higher sugar content, will get tough and too dark if left in the machine after completion.

DIRTY DANCING - *Keep your machine in its place.*

The Problem: Heavier doughs and extended kneading times may make your machine vibrate on the counter. We've even had a few dance off the counter during an overnight time bake!
What To Do:
- Be sure your machine is on a firm, level surface well away from the edge.

HOCKEY PUCKS - *And loaves of the shorter persuasion*

The Problem: Your loaf looks like a hockey puck.
What To Do:
- You forgot your yeast. Remember it next time, this loaf is history.

The Problem: The loaf is slightly higher, like a hockey puck on steroids.
What To Do:
- In general, a "two-hour" or rapid cycle will produce a shorter, denser loaf than a longer cycle. This is especially true with complex recipes.

Controlled test bake without yeast.

- Some stone ground and whole wheat flours will bake a shorter loaf, but not a puck.
- Water that is either too hot or too cold is a yeast inhibitor. Think tepid, "like a baby's bath … "
- Hard tap water may cause short loaves. To fix this, add one teaspoon of lemon juice or vinegar per cup of water.
- Another possibility: You accidentally added too much salt.
- Your yeast may be old. Test it by mixing one teaspoon of sugar and one tablespoon of yeast in one half cup of warm water. If the mixture doubles in volume in 15 minutes, the yeast is still good.

ON THE STREET WHERE YOU LIVE - *Correcting for local conditions*

Needless to say, summers in Anchorage, Alaska, are different than summers in Albuquerque or Atlanta. Humidity, temperature, and water quality can affect your bread results. For instance, yeast may process faster in hot weather, so you may need less. In humid weather, heavier flours may absorb the moisture in the air more than finer, softer flours.

We've told you what we discovered about the variables of flour, water and yeast, but you'll be the expert on *your* ingredients in *your* machine in *your* climate.

ACCESSORIES

BERRIES AND CHERRIES
- Savor the taste of summer all year long. These Chukar brand dried fruits transform simple fruit bread into something special. Packed in a resealable bag. One pound Berry Medley of strawberries, blueberries and cranberries, $15. Cherries, $11. Cranberries only $8.

SLICING SIMPLICITY - Want a knife that glides through a hot loaf? This 10" bread knife is the best we've found! Use it with the beechwood bread slicer to produce uniform 1/2" slices for sandwiches and toast every time.
Knife $21.95, Slicer $12.95

TOOL FOR TROUBLESOME TASK - Does your kneading blade stick in your loaf? The test kitchen used needle-nosed pliers until we had these. One flip of the wrist and our wooden bread hook liberates the blade without mauling your loaf or burning your fingers. $4.

STORE, SEE AND SERVE -This jumbo bread box lets you view what's in store. The durable, clear cover opens from either side. Use as a bread serving tray from the countertop to the table, $25.

LEATHER MITTS -Tired of dropping the pan when shaking out the loaf? Here's our test kitchen's solution. Imagine a soft, supple mitt with a firm grip, impervious to singes. Machine washable too! New longer length mitts protect the entire forearm against burns from larger capacity pans and call also be used for grilling.

Regular mitts in hunter green, red, taupe, cobalt blue and black. $30 a pair.
Extra long, in green or blue. $35 a pair.

HEAVY DUTY, LIGHT WEIGHT
These stylish, crystal clear canisters look like glass, but they're actually feather-light acrylic. The large pail holds a 5 lb. bag of flour; buy one pail for white and one for whole wheat. Add the 4-piece canister set for sugar, salt, dry milk, and yeast, and you will have our 6-piece "Bread Baker's Bunch."

Large Pail, $40;
Two Pails, $70;
Canister Set, $50;
Baker's Bunch, $95.

MILL YOUR OWN - Venture into the freshest ingredients possible with this easy to use, 3 cup capacity grain mill from Regal. Numerous settings from coarsely cracked to finely ground. $49.99.

WARM AND BEAUTIFUL - Keep your bread warm at the table in a portable basket heated by a microwaveable heating pouch. Hunter Green or Burgundy, $32.95.

Accessory Hotline
1-800-541-2733

CUTE COVER-UPS - Why put your machine away when these washable covers can make it part of the decor? Designed to fit all machines, choose ivory with green or blue trim; or blue floral.

Solid colors	$20
Floral pattern	$22

ALASKAN SOURDOUGH KIT - If we could package the history, flavor and romance of the 49th state, this is how we'd do it. The starter has been passed down in Alaska since 1919, and was used by Ruth Allman, author of "Alaska Sourdough," the charming anecdote-filled guide of an Alaskan pioneer. Since it arrival in our Anchorage test kitchen, Tom's hearty starter has produced flavorful bread machine loaves. The 2-cup jar hand crafted by Tom's Pots is the perfect size to refrigerate sourdough. Tom's Starter jar, $22; Ruth's Cookbook, $10; or the Alaskan Kit, $30.

ADJUSTABLE SPOONS - Tired of juggling those little engraved measuring spoons like a charm bracelet to find the one you want? These adjustable spoons not only end the juggling forever, they feature such hard to find measurements as 1/8, 1 1/2 and 2 1/2 teaspoons. Accurate and dishwasher safe. Set, $6.95.

CONQUER MEASURING

This kit will get you started and keep you accurate from dry to wet for years to come. **Get everything on this page, a $27 value, for only $20.**

THE WONDER CUP - Used in our test kitchen every day, this unique 2 cup measurer is simple in design and operation, but detailed in measurement, $8.

CLEARLY CORRECT -At our request, our friends at Emsa Frieling created the "Perfect Beaker" for liquid measurement. Uniquely shaped, the two cup capacity beaker is designed with lots of markings to ensure accuracy - cups, tablespoons, teaspoons, even metric! You'll love this easy-to-see measuring experience. $6.

CONTEMPORARY MEASURES -Stylish but sturdy, this set of measuring cups is accurate and dishwasher safe with easy-to-read markings. Measuring cups, $5 for the set.

FLOUR LEVELER - This is the best $1.50 you'll ever spend for accurately measured ingredients. This bowl scraper is perfect to level off your dry ingredients for a true measure.

BASKET OF BOUNTY -Fascinated by our recipes, but can't find all the ingredients? Search no more! Our basket includes garlic, pesto and tomato pastes, SAF and Bakipan yeasts, wheat gluten, coconut milk, wheat germ, cracked wheat, bran flakes, 7-Grain cereal and Cajun spice. Individual yeasts $5; other ingredients, $4; any three items for $10; or the entire Basket of Bounty $49.95.

Giving a gift? Send the Basket of Bounty with a copy of *Electric Bread*, $69.95.

SIMPLE STORAGE - Here's an inexpensive way to keep your flour fresh and dry. A set of plastic storage bins, perfectly sized for 5 lb. and 10 lb. bags of flour. $12 for the Set.

Accessory Hotline
1-800-541-2733

FRESH SLICES -This product combines bread storage with a convenient slicing tray that can also be used for serving. The canister keeps fresh bread airtight. Microwave, freezer and dishwasher safe - $15.

FOR A CLEAN MACHINE - These scrub mitts are great! The blue side safely works on the machine interior, while the yellow side takes care of cleaning the non-stick pan without damage. 2 mitts for $5.

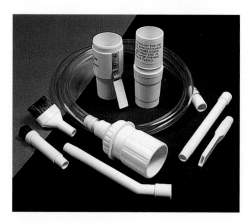

The Mini Attachments turn your vacuum hose into a miniature powerhouse with flexible tubing, crevice and brush tools.
Great for typewriters and computers; too! $13.

JUMBO CROCK & SOURDOUGH -

Strike it rich right there in your kitchen! This 7-cup capacity sourdough crock attractively stores the bubbling sourdough. The possibilities are endless for customizing your own breads. For starters, choose Tom's, $5; or Goldrush, $3; complete your selection with the large hand-crafted crock, $20.

COZY BREAD KEEPERS - Just the thing
for your country kitchen, these washable cotton bags hold any size loaf. They make great gift bags for house warmings. Available in blue, green or black with wooden ring closure. $9.

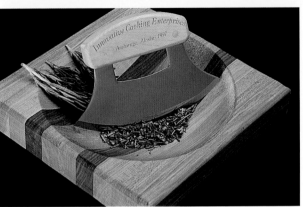

BLADE, BLOCK AND ULU - Used for centuries by native people of the arctic, the ulu (pronounced ooloo) increases dexterity and leverage to make fine cuts simple and heavy chopping easier. The accompanying solid walnut and birch bowl is shaped to fit the ulu blade on one side and is a chopping block on the other. An ideal gift for yourself or that special someone, $34.95.

MORE ELECTRIC BREAD® - As
beautiful and flavorful as *Electric Bread*, this sequel brings you all <u>new</u> recipes in a totally new ring binder format. Gourmet recipes like Espresso, Millet and Thai combine with sections on bagels, focaccia and sweet rolls. Pages of full-color dough techniques show you how to form any bread machine dough into easy and elegant shapes. There's even a recipe storage pouch. *More Electric Bread* - the next step of your bread machine adventure. $29.95.

INDEX

Introducing MORE ELECTRIC BREAD®

and More....

and More....

and More....

ALL NEW RECIPES FOR PEOPLE WITH MORE TASTE THAN TIME

More Electric Bread takes you beyond the basics with all new recipes and even more specialty doughs in a new ring binder format:

- *Only in the Machine* **contains** 32 new gourmet breads;
- *Rolled and Pulled* delivers 22 basic recipes and techniques for bagels, focaccia and rolls; and
- in *Extras*, you'll find 15 full-color dough techniques to roll and form **any** bread machine dough into easy and elegant shapes.

Gourmet Breads:
Three Seeds
Tomato Basil
Very Berry
Whole Wheat Spice
Wild Rice
Zesty Orange
Olive
Onion Walnut
Pepper Corn
Portuguese Sweet
Reuben, Reuben
Rice Pudding
Smoky Almond
Spicy Beef
Sweet Ho Yin
Thai Bread
Cheezy Ranch
Chocolate
Cinnamon Sunrise
Corn Fritter
Creamy Rye
Espresso
French Wheat
Garlic Blues
Holiday Cranberry
Home Style White
Irish Soda
Jodi's Rum Cake

Kugelhopf
Maple Walnut
Mexican Sunset
Millet

Bagels:
Basic
Cheese
Cinnamon Raisin
Cranberry Orange
Garlic
Onion
Pumpkin Spice
Whole Wheat

Focaccia:
Ambrosia
Apple
Basic w/Garlic-Herb
Rosemary Cheese
Simple
Sun Dried Tomato
Sweet Pepper
Tomato & Onion

Sweet Rolls:
Apple
Cinnamon Rolls
Cherry
Orange
Peanut Butter
Raspberry

Our Test Kitchen

*No one has baked more bread in more machines than our test kitchen. Now, with **More Electric Bread**, you can take that next step for the adventuresome bread machine owners!*

Available at gourmet and retail stores or by calling 1-800-541-2733.

159

We gratefully acknowledge our friends and loved ones who have given us the advice, encouragement and confidence needed to make Electric Bread a phenomenal success. They fed our dreams and our children, while we tested recipes and, too often, patience.

Some have moved on, and are fondly remembered. Others continue to generously contribute their ideas, energy and talents. We sincerely thank each person who has made our books and our lives better, whether through grand sacrifices or small gestures. Without this "cast of hundreds," running Innovative Cooking Enterprises, Inc., might seem like work.

Electric Bread Second Edition Team:

Test Kitchen
- Executive Chefs -
Greg Forte, C.E.C., C.C.E.
Tim Doebler, C.W.C., C.C.E.
- Operations Manager -
Jon Roberts
- Technicians -
Renie Brandow
Mary Ann Swalling
Vonda Nixon
Cecilia Slay

Manufacturer Co-ordination
Lara Parrish

Technical Assistance
Color Art Printing
Mary Jo Exley
Lanrie Leung
John McKay
Oleg Parshin
Donna Alderman
April Carter
Jim Dobbelaire
Amy Fitzpatrick
Jill Kolberg
Debra Ann Schneider
Jonell Snook-Holmes

Management
Ann Parrish
Shirley Laird
Chris Swalling
Patti McBride